Toft cottage weavery

Mabry Mill

Echoview Fiber Mill

River Arts District

Black Mountain Yarn Shop

Asheville

North Carolina

Founder/Creator, Author and Creative Director: Andrea Hungerford
Photographer and Editor: Karen DeWitz
Pattern Designers: Mara Catherine Bryner, Andrea Hungerford, Sarah Pope
Models: Emmersen Cohn, Andrea Hungerford, Katie Porter
Recipe: Karen DeWitz
Patterns Technical Editor: Meaghan Corwin and Alexandra Viegel
Marketing and Social Media: Hannah Thiessen
Map Artist: Peggy Dean
Printer: B&B Print Source

ORDERING INFORMATION
By Hand is published three times annually. Subscriptions or single-issue
purchases can be ordered online at: www.byhandserial.com.

Wholesale inquiries may be submitted via e-mail to www.nnkpress.com.

Published by Blueberry Hill
www.byhandserial.com
info@byhandserial.com

PRINTED IN THE USA
This book is printed on Forest Stewardship Council® certified paper.
FSC® certification ensures that the paper in this publication contains
fibers from well managed and responsibly harvested forests that meet
strict environmental and socioeconomic standards.

FIRST EDITION
Spring 2018

Cover photo: The view across the rolling foothills of the Blue Ridge Mountains in southwestern Virginia.
Opposite page: Pink dogwoods in bloom welcome springtime to the South.

By Hand
making communities

Lookbook No. 6: Blue Ridge Mountains

Table Of Contents

The Blue Ridge Mountains of
Western North Carolina and Virginia 1

Making Communities 2

LYS: Black Mountain Yarn Shop 5

Knitting Pattern:
Seven Sisters Yoked Pullover 10

Shepherding:
Cestari Sheep & Wool Company 19

Soapmaking: Essential Journeys 25

Locally Produced:
Echoview Fiber Mill 31

Knitting Pattern:
Allegheny Pullover Hoodie 34

Hand Dyed Speckles: Junkyarn 41

Knitting Pattern:
The Kemper Wrap 44

On the Loom:
Toft Cottage Weavery 49

Knitwear Design: Appalachian Knits 53

Hand Crafting Project:
Luminous Yarn Lights 56

Woodworking: Ray Jones
Woodcrafts 61

Sewing: Vesta Patterns 65

Sewing Project: Maywood Totepack 68

In the Kitchen: Spring Clouds 79

Surface Design:
Cloth Fiber Workshop 82

Where to Learn:
Penland School of Crafts 85

Opposite page: The Blue Ridge Mountains of southwest Virginia.

The Blue Ridge Mountains of Western North Carolina and Virginia

Often, in travel and in life, it's the small moments - rather than a big "aha" event - that make up the sum of our experiences. It's small moments that brought me joy and a sense of place while traveling through the Blue Ridge Mountains. Watching Whitney Hills' beehives buzzing with activity - from a cautious distance - while she explained that the electric fence was to keep out a mama bear and her three cubs who wandered into her yard most days. Pondering the almost endless selection of delicious tacos at White Duck Taco Shop every day for lunch. Standing at the fenceline on one of the Blue Ridge Parkway's many turnouts, no one else in sight and no sound but the wind, looking out into the vast forested wildness spread out in a panorama before me. Eating brownies and salted caramel ice cream while looking out the big plate glass window at French Broad Chocolates, watching the evening unfold in Pack Square. Breathing in the scent of fresh hay and watching the sun shining on newborn lambs, turning their big ears a glowing pink. Chatting with the friendly barista at the Dripolator, a small, cozy coffeehouse next door to Black Mountain Yarn Shop that serves the best apple walnut bread I've ever tasted. Watching artists quietly at work in the big, light-filled studios at Penland School of Crafts, envying them their focus and intensity of purpose. Strolling amongst the historical buildings of Staunton, Virginia, enjoying the small-town ambiance and the friendly people in all of the restaurants and shops. Wandering through the warehouses of the River Arts District in Asheville, marveling at the gigantic murals and peeking in on artists at work. This is what evokes for me what it feels like to travel through the Blue Ridge Mountains, from the high peaks of North Carolina up into the rolling hills of Virginia. What a beautiful, inspiring place to work, play, and create! ⌘

Making Communities

The lives of many of the people I meet on my travels are so different from my own, it can be hard for me to grasp what it must be like to walk in their shoes. The frequent solitude and hard outdoor work of a sheep farmer bears no resemblance to my helter-skelter days spent mostly in the car, driving my daughters to and from all of their classes and activities. The vagabond life of a writer and designer who, although nearly half my age, has already moved over 40 times and has the gumption and freedom to reshape her life as many times as she wants, stands in stark contrast to the country home my family built and has lived in for almost 20 years, and my practice of law for over two decades. The daily routine of a retired weaver who has made her home in a sleepy village, far down a country road where little has changed over the years, is hard for me to imagine as I fight rush hour traffic and navigate a city where over half a million people live. And it's difficult for me to comprehend the life experiences of an artist who has bicycled all over the United States—and the world—ever since she finished college.

Sometimes, it seems like our lives are all so different that there are almost no points of commonality, and the differences make it seem as if it would be impossible to relate to or understand each other. But the one point of reference we all have is a love of and respect for making. Time and again, I find that shared value to be overwhelmingly powerful. Discussing the passion inspired by handwork, the joy of finding a creative outlet, the importance of honoring and respecting traditions while at the same time finding new and innovative ways to express time-honored crafts—all of these create a shared language that transcends a world of differences.

Now, more than ever, we need ways to find common ground between people. Now, when it seems that more divides us than unites us, our ability to celebrate a shared experience is crucial. As shepherd extraordinaire Francis Chester said as we watched his newborn lambs, "If everyone in the world learned to knit or crochet or weave or spin or felt, there would be no wars."

We may not be pursuing our love of hand crafts in order to bring about world peace, but it does give us all the opportunity to create a shared frame of reference with others who we might otherwise never know. Whether at our local knitting store or craft guild, while attending a retreat, virtually through online groups and chats, or even just by reading about the artists in **By Hand**, making broadens our circle and allows us to find common ground.

So who knows? Maybe making by hand will save the world. At the least, it will give all of us a chance to meet, interact with, get to know, and perhaps even befriend people from different walks of life, and to share the joy we all find in creative expression. ⌘

Warmly,

Andrea

Opposite page: Marveling at the largest tree in Asheville's Beaver Lake Bird Sanctuary.

Springtime brings out the wildlife and wisteria blossoms in Staunton, Virginia.

4

LYS: Black Mountain Yarn Shop

Black Mountain Yarn Shop is a paradise for lovers of hand dyed yarns. The selection of well-known indie dyers is extensive. For instance, one of the first things you see when you enter is an entire cabinet full of Hedgehog Fibers. Just as wonderful is the opportunity to discover new indie dyers, who bring innovative methods and hues to speckles and hand dyes: Old Soul Fiber Co. from South Carolina, fellow North Carolinian Junkyarn, and then farther flung, difficult-to-find yarns like Ireland's Life in the Long Grass, Miss La Motte from South Africa, and French yarn Tot Le Matin. Shop owners and husband and wife team Don and Donna Farrow do a lot of research in order to bring their customers unique yarns of the best possible quality. "We love hand dyed yarns and our customers love them, too," explains Donna. And the options don't stop at indie dyed yarns. Knitters can find entire lines from Brooklyn Tweed, Woolfolk, Quince & Co, Rosy Green Wool, YOTH, and Madelinetosh, just to name a few.

A fantastic yarn selection is not the only draw, though. Customers come from far and wide for the warm and inviting friendliness with which everyone through the door is greeted. Ever since Don and Donna moved to the small, bucolic town of Black Mountain and opened the shop nine years ago, their primary purpose has been to build community. "It's just amazing to us, every day we feel so blessed about how people are so supportive of us," smiles Donna. Don adds that, "we wanted to give back to the community that was good to us. Our shop not only gives back to the community, it creates community here in the store."

The classes and activities at Black Mountain are almost too many to enumerate: morning knitting groups, regular knitting and crochet clinics, KALs that meet weekly, classes taught by local teachers, and special guests

like Stephen West and Andrea Mowry. The shop regularly draws customers from Georgia, Tennessee, South Carolina, Virginia, and vacationers from all over the country. Although there is no online store, many customers call in, and orders are shipped out almost daily. Donna also organizes "knit-away trips" that travel to knitworthy destinations. Two years ago, a group of 15 knitters traveled to Chicago, and last year an even larger group traveled to Maine to stay in Camden, tour Swans Island Company, and visit Portland LYS Knitwit.

"Our customers are such a great group," Donna tells me. "If our ladies are sitting here and a stranger comes in, they engage them in conversation. They're so much a part of us, because they want everybody to feel as welcome as we do. I love the yarn, but I really love our people." Both Don and Donna knit, as do their two employees, and they're always ready to provide help or advice, as well as a particularly warm welcome for new knitters. "It can be intimidating walking into a yarn shop, so we really strive to make everybody feel welcome," Donna explains.

Visiting Black Mountain gives customers a chance to experience the charm of the historic town as well. The building where the shop is located was built in the 1920s and used to house a Chevy garage, although it has since been renovated into a bright, airy space with lots of natural light. It is surrounded by small, independent businesses—many of which are also owned by husband and wife teams—where visitors can shop and eat. Don and Donna love to make recommendations and help anyone new to town experience the small-town charm that Don says "is like living in Mayberry." ⌘

Yarn Contents:	100% Superwash Merino
Care Instructions:	Hand wash, cool water, dry flat
Yardage:	Approximately 560 yards, 4.0 oz, 113g
ID/Color:	Black Mountain Yarn Shop

~ A special color for a special yarn shop ~

Fifty Shades of Gradient™

the fibre studio
at yarns to dye for

thefibrestudio.com

Black Mountain Yarn Shop

Owners: Donna and Don Farrow

Website:
blackmountainyarnshop.com

Address: 203 W. State St., Black Mountain, N.C.

Phone: 828.669.7570

Travelers most often imagine the Blue Ridge Mountains with a wide view, standing at a viewpoint looking out over miles of rolling hills and wild country. Surprisingly, the mountains are also lovely viewed close up, offering a surprising bounty of beautiful wildflowers from the early spring through the fall.

Since this region was never frozen in the last ice age, many of the flowers that died out under advancing glaciers to the north continued to flourish here. The result is one of the most diverse and flower strewn natural areas in the United States. The Blue Ridge Parkway, a 469-mile scenic drive through the Appalachian Highlands, boasts

Top: Elliott's blueberry
Middle: Purple phacelia
Bottom: Carolina phlox

Wildflowers

nearly 1300 different species of flowering plants. You can find tiny blue-eyed grass and violets all the way up to huge wild rhododendrons and flowering trees.

If hiking through backcountry trails doesn't suit you, or if you just want a way to browse a variety of species in one place, many of these native flowers can also be found at the Botanical Gardens at Asheville. In this ten-acre non-profit garden, you can wind your way through natural landscapes of carefully preserved native flora and fauna. They offer a variety of classes to educate and guide people in understanding and preserving the native plants of the area.

Top: Rosebay rhododendron
Middle: Sweet William phlox
Bottom: Virginia bluebells

Seven Sisters
Yoked Pullover by Sarah Pope

This pullover is worked in the round from the bottom up, with a mantle of stars decorating the circular yoke. The star motifs, worked in purls and traveling stitches, are adapted from a traditional Danish design catalogued by Vivian Høxbro, but my choice to place them in a ring below the neckline is influenced by Shetland yoke patterning. The effect also reminds me of an American quilt pattern with clustered stars known as Seven Stars or Seven Sisters—perhaps in reference to the Pleiades in Greek mythology and astronomy. The name seemed fitting in homage to quilting as an important art form in the Blue Ridge Mountains.

SIZES
XXS (XS, S, M, L, XL, 2XL)
Shown in size XS
Intended to be worn with 2–4" of ease

FINISHED MEASUREMENTS
Bust circumference 34.5 (36.25, 39.25, 41.75, 44.75, 47.25, 49.75)"
Length from back neck 23.75 (23.75, 24.25, 24.75, 25.25, 25.25, 25.75)"

MATERIALS
Cestari Ash Lawn Collection 3 Ply DK weight (75% cotton/25% wool, 250 yds per 100 g), 5 (5, 5, 6, 6, 6, 7) skeins in Blue Denim, or approximately 1040 (1100, 1175, 1265, 1340, 1415, 1505) yards

US 4 (3.5 mm) 24" circular needle and set of DPNs (tubular CO)
US 6 (4 mm) 24" or 32" circular needle and set of DPNs (body and sleeves)
US 3 (3.25 mm) 16" circular needle (neckband)
Tapestry needle, stitch markers, stitch holders, waste yarn

GAUGE
22 sts and 28 rows = 4" in stockinette stitch with US 6 (4 mm) needles, blocked

NOTES
Body and sleeves are worked in the round to the underarm, then joined and the yoke worked in one piece to the neck. Body has vertical darts for waist shaping.

Short rows are used several times in the body and yoke to lengthen the back of the pullover.

Yoke pattern is worked from a chart. Read all rounds from right to left, paying attention to beginning and ending points for your size.

BODY
Cast On Option I (Tubular CO):
Using US 4 (3.5 mm) circular needle and waste yarn, CO 96 (101, 109, 116, 124, 131, 138) sts with any method. Change to working yarn.
Row 1 (WS): Purl.
Row 2 (RS): *K1, lift running thread between sts from front to back with left needle tip and purl this new st; rep from * to last 2 sts, k1, lift running thread, purl running thread together with last st. Pm and join to work in the round, being careful not to twist. 190 (200, 216, 230, 246, 260, 274) sts.
Rnd 3: *Sl 1 pwise wyib, p1; rep from * to end.
Rnd 4: *K1, sl 1 pwise wyif; rep from * to end.
Rnd 5: Repeat Rnd 3.
Change to US 6 (4 mm) needle.

Cast On Option II (Knitter's Choice):
Using US 6 (4 mm) circular needle and working yarn, CO 190 (200, 216, 230, 246, 260, 274) sts using your preferred elastic method. Pm and join to work in the round, being careful not to twist.

Both Options Continue:
Work in k1, p1 rib for 10 rnds.

Change to stockinette st. Work 9 rnds even.

Short-Row Shaping:
Short Row 1 (RS): K95 (100, 108, 115, 123, 130, 137), pm for side, knit to last st, w&t.

Short Row 2 (WS): Purl to 1 st before side m, w&t.
Short Row 3: Knit to 6 sts before previous wrapped st, w&t.
Short Row 4: Purl to 6 sts before previous wrapped st, w&t.
Short Row 5: Knit to end of round, picking up and knitting wraps together with wrapped sts as you encounter them.
Next Rnd: Knit to end, picking up and knitting remaining wraps together with wrapped sts.
Work 4 rnds even.

Shape Waist
Next Rnd: K24 (25, 27, 29, 31, 33, 34), pm for dart, k47 (50, 54, 57, 61, 64, 69), pm for dart, k24 (25, 27, 29, 31, 33, 34), sl side m, k32 (33, 36, 38, 41, 43, 46), pm for dart, k31 (34, 36, 39, 41, 44, 45), pm for dart, k32 (33, 36, 38, 41, 43, 46).

Waist Dec Rnd: [Knit to 2 sts before dart m, ssk, sl m, knit to next dart m, sl m, k2tog] 2 times, knit to end. 4 sts dec'd.
Repeat Waist Dec Rnd on every 12th rnd 2 more times. 178 (188, 204, 218, 234, 248, 262) sts rem.

Work 12 rnds even.

Waist Inc Rnd: [Knit to 1 st before dart m, Inv-R, sl m, knit to next dart m, sl m, Inv-L] 2 times, knit to end. 4 sts inc'd.
Repeat Waist Inc Rnd on every 14th rnd 2 more times. 190 (200, 216, 230, 246, 260, 274) sts.

Remove dart m and work even until piece measures 15'' from CO (measured at beg

of rnd m, not over short rows) or desired length to underarm, ending last rnd 5 (5, 6, 6, 8, 8, 10) sts before beg-of-rnd m.

Division Rnd: *K9 (9, 11, 12, 16, 16, 19), then place these sts on waste yarn or stitch holder for left underarm, removing m. Knit across front to side m, sl m, k4 (4, 5, 6, 8, 8, 9), then place the previous 9 (9, 11, 12, 16, 16, 19) sts on waste yarn or holder for right underarm, removing m. Knit across back to end. 86 (91, 97, 103, 107, 114, 118) sts rem for front and for back.

Do not break yarn. Set body aside and work sleeves.

SLEEVES
Option I (Tubular CO):
Using US 4 (3.5 mm) circular needle and waste yarn, CO 23 (23, 23, 24, 25, 26, 27) sts with any method. Change to working yarn. Work Rows 1 & 2 as for body tubular CO. You will have 44 (44, 44, 46, 48, 50, 52) sts. Divide sts evenly over US 4 (3.5 mm) DPNs, pm and join to work in the round, being careful not to twist. Work Rnds 3–5 as for body tubular CO.
Change to US 6 (4 mm) DPNs.

Option II (Knitter's Choice):
Using US 6 (4 mm) DPNs and working yarn, CO 44 (44, 44, 46, 48, 50, 52) sts using your preferred elastic method. Pm and join to work in the round, being careful not to twist.

Both Options Continue:
Work in k1, p1 rib for 8 rnds.
Change to stockinette st and work 17 (17, 17, 17, 17, 17, 13) rnds even.

Shape Sleeve:

Sleeve Increase Rnd 1: Knit to last 3 sts, Inv-R, knit to end. 1 st inc'd.

Sleeve Increase Rnd 2: K2, Inv-L, knit to end. 1 st inc'd.

Work 6 (6, 5, 5, 4, 4, 4) rnds even.

Repeat the last 8 (8, 7, 7, 6, 6, 6) rnds 11 (11, 13, 13, 15, 15, 17) more times. 68 (68, 72, 74, 80, 82, 88) sts.

Work even until sleeve measures 18.5 (18.5, 19, 19, 19, 19, 19)" from CO or desired length to underarm, ending last rnd 5 (5, 6, 6, 8, 8, 10) sts before the m.

Next Rnd: K9 (9, 11, 12, 16, 16, 19) then place these sts on a holder or waste yarn for underarm, removing m. Break yarn and transfer remaining 59 (59, 61, 62, 64, 66, 69) live sts to waste yarn or a spare needle.

Work a second sleeve to match the first.

YOKE

Joining Rnd: Take up sweater body and replace beg-of-rnd m on right needle tip, at left edge of back sts. Using yarn attached to body, k59 (59, 61, 62, 64, 66, 69) sts of first sleeve, pm for left front, knit across front sts decreasing 1 (2, 1, 0, 1, 0, 0) sts(s) evenly spaced, pm for right front, k59 (59, 61, 62, 64,

66, 69) sts of second sleeve, knit across back sts decreasing 1 (1, 0, 0, 1, 0, 0) st(s) evenly spaced. [2 (3, 1, 0, 2, 0, 0) st(s) dec'd in total.] 288 (297, 315, 330, 340, 360, 374) sts on needle.

Short-Row Shaping:
Short Row 1 (RS): Knit to left front m, sl m, w&t.
Short Row 2 (WS): Purl past beg-of-rnd m to right front m, sl m, w&t.
Short Row 3: Knit to 6 sts before previously wrapped st, w&t.
Short Row 4: Purl to 6 sts before previously wrapped st, w&t.
Short Rows 5 & 6: Repeat Short Rows 3 & 4.
Short Row 7: Knit to beg-of-rnd m.
Next Rnd: Knit to end of rnd, picking up and knitting wraps together with wrapped sts as you encounter them.

Work 7 (7, 9, 10, 12, 12, 14) rnds even, ending last rnd 43 (45, 49, 51, 53, 57, 59) sts before beg-of-rnd m. You are at center back, which will be the beginning of the round from now on. Shift the beg-of-rnd m to this point. Note: Leave left & right front markers in place for final short-row shaping.

Yoke Pattern:
Work Rnds 1–26 of Yoke Chart. After chart is complete, 208 (207, 225, 230, 240, 260, 264) sts rem.

Shape Yoke:
Work 6 (6, 7, 10, 11, 11, 13) rnds even.
Next Rnd: Knit, decreasing 4 (3, 3, 0, 2, 0) sts evenly spaced. 204 (204, 222, 228, 240, 258, 264) sts rem.
Yoke Dec Rnd: *K1, k2tog; rep from * to end. 136 (136, 148, 152, 160, 172, 176) sts rem.

Wrapped Stitches:
Rnd 1: *Wrap 2 sts (bring yarn to front, sl 2 to right needle, bring yarn to back, sl 2 back to left needle, bring yarn to front, sl same 2 sts to right needle, bring yarn to back), k2; rep from * to end.
Rnd 2: Knit, adjusting wrap tension as needed by inserting the needle tip under the strands and gently tugging them outward from the face of the fabric.
Rnd 3: *K2, wrap 2 sts; rep from *.
Rnd 4: Knit, adjusting wrap tension as needed.

Short-Row Shaping:
Short Row 1 (RS): Knit to left front m, sl m, w&t.
Short Row 2 (WS): Purl past beg-of-rnd m to right front m, sl m, w&t.
Short Row 3: Knit to 6 sts before previously wrapped st, w&t.
Short Row 4: Purl to 6 sts before previously wrapped st, w&t.
Short Row 5: Knit to beg-of-rnd m.
Next Rnd: Knit to end of rnd, picking up and knitting wraps together with wrapped sts as you encounter them.

BO all sts knitwise and somewhat firmly to stabilize neckline.

NECKBAND
Using US 3 (3.25 mm) needle, with RS facing pick up and knit 1 st in each purl bump, just inside the BO round. 136 (136, 148, 152, 160, 172, 176) sts. Pm for beg of rnd. Purl 3 rnds. BO all sts pwise.

FINISHING
Graft underarm stitches and weave in ends. Remove waste yarn from the tubular CO edges. Wet block finished sweater to schematic measurements.

ABBREVIATIONS
BO – bind off, bound–off
CC – contrast color
CO – cast on, cast–on
Dec('d) – decrease(d)
Inc('d) – increase(d)
Inv-L – invisible left increase: sl next st pwise with yarn in back, then place the left leg of the st in the row below the slipped st on the left needle and knit it
Inv-R – invisible right increase: place the right leg of the st in the row below next st onto left needle and knit it, then sl next st pwise with yarn in back
K – knit
K2tog – knit 2 sts together
K3tog – knit 3 sts together
M – marker
MC – main color
P – purl
P2tog – purl 2 sts together
Pm – place marker
Pwise – purlwise/as if to purl
Rem – remain
Rep – repeat
Rnd(s) – round(s)
RS – right side
Sl – slip
Ssk – [sl 1 as if to knit] 2 times, insert left needle into fronts of these 2 sts and knit them together
Sssk – [sl 1 as if to knit] 3 times, insert left needle into fronts of these 3 sts and knit them together
St(s) – stitch(es)
St st – stockinette stitch
W&t – wrap and turn (see Techniques)
WS – wrong side

24.75 (24.75, 27, 27.75, 29, 31.25, 32)"

12.25 (12.25, 13, 13.5, 14.5, 15, 16)"

2"

6.75 (6.75, 7.25, 7.75, 8.25, 8.25, 8.75)"

18.5 (18.5, 19, 19, 19, 19, 19)"

32.25 (34.25, 37, 39.75, 42.5, 45, 47.75)"

15"

8 (8, 8, 8.25, 8.75, 9, 9.5)"

34.5 (36.25, 39.25, 41.75, 44.75, 47.25, 49.75)"

TECHNIQUES
Wrap and Turn for Short Rows (w&t)
On a RS row: Slip the next st pwise wyib, bring yarn to front between needles, return slipped st to left needle, turn work.

On a WS row: Slip the next st pwise wyif, bring yarn to back between needles, return slipped st to left needle, turn work.

YOKE CHART

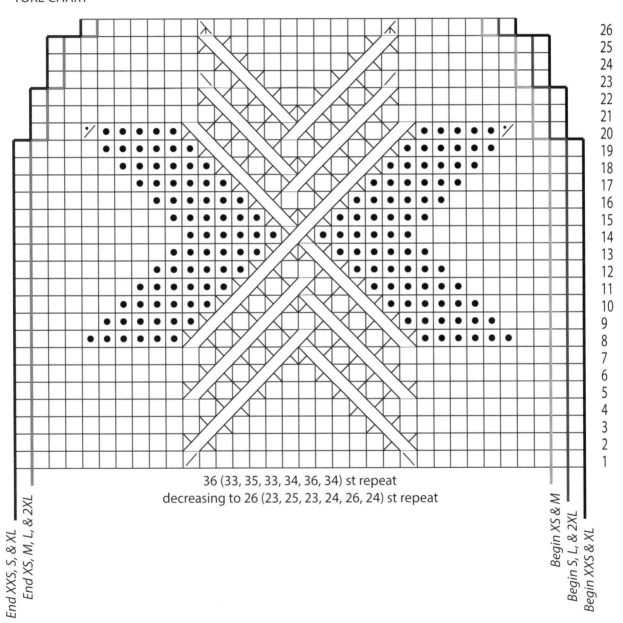

36 (33, 35, 33, 34, 36, 34) st repeat
decreasing to 26 (23, 25, 23, 24, 26, 24) st repeat

End XXS, S, & XL
End XS, M, L, & 2XL

Begin XS & M
Begin S, L, & 2XL
Begin XXS & XL

Shepherding: Cestari Sheep & Wool Company

Francis Chester is a born storyteller, as anyone who has had the pleasure of sitting down with him for a chat will likely tell you. A lifetime of fascinating anecdotes, punctuated with his great booming laugh, immediately put you at ease and draw you in.

Francis' family history is wonderfully rich and is deeply embedded in the world of sheep and textiles. Both of his parents were born in Italy, and his father's side of the family raised sheep there for centuries. "I have shepherding in my blood," he explains, and then launches into an enthralling story about how his forebears learned to defend their flock from wolves and bears with nothing more than rocks to throw —much like the story of David and Goliath. His mother's family owned textile plants in New York, and his great-grandmother spun linen and wool in Italy, which is the inspiration for a new line of yarn he's working on that he says will be "the best of the old and the best of today."

Shepherding and farming has been Francis' passion since he was a young boy. He started his farm stand on Long Island when he was ten years old. "It [Long Island] was mostly farms then, more than in Virginia. I had a farm in Oyster Bay, and I raised sheep—I was about the only sheep farmer on Long Island." It was at an early age, Francis says, that "I fell in love with sheep. There is a relationship between the shepherd and the sheep. Sheep have a personality—you can feel a connection with them. When the cowboys [who herd cattle] tell me that sheep are dumb, that just burns me up. If you want to know where the water is, turn the sheep out—if there's water, they'll find it. Sheep can remember two years later individual people or other sheep. I can take my lambs and pull them out, leave them a day away from their mothers, then bring them back, and within 20 minutes, the babies and mothers will find each other."

Although Francis' passion was shepherding and farming, at his father's urging, he chose lawyering as a "back-up plan." He had many relatives on his mother's side who were lawyers and judges, so he reluctantly entered law school, and opened his own practice after graduation. As a small-town lawyer, Francis practices general law and ends up with all types of legal work. He regales me with a story of representing a man accused of assassinating a sitting judge, and the threads of racial tensions, insanity pleas, and a hung jury keep me on the edge of my seat. Then he shows me a gift from one of his clients—a briefcase with an engraved label that reads: "Enjoys a good fight and isn't afraid of contempt of court"—and he laughs as he launches into another story of a hard-fought legal battle.

In 1968, Francis and his wife moved to Virginia. "When I came to Virginia, they were offering almost nothing for wool," Francis remembers. "I decided to go to New England, and found a mill for our fleeces in Maine. My wife and I would skein and label the yarn, and then I'd take it to Maryland and Washington, D.C. I didn't know that much about yarn—I knew sheep, but not yarn. I sold everything I had with me in two weeks, and made some good friends who taught me about knitting and crocheting. This was in the late 1960s. Then the mills started closing in the 1970s, and all the wool was being sent to China, so I decided to buy a mill." Many of Francis' skills and abilities are self-taught, and this was no exception. He learned the nomenclature, watched and learned in the New England mills, and went from mill to mill buying used machinery, building up his equipment. "I started learning what I needed, put it all together and sent it down to Virginia, and we built our first mill in 1980. It went online in 1981, and it was a dream."

Next comes stories of awards won and booming business, punctuated with hard financial times, the loss of almost everything, and then slowly rebuilding to the current day, with a growing business and ambitious plans for expansion in the works. A majestic new mill, with many times the capacity of the current mill, is in the process of being built. We tour the foundation as Francis explains what each section of the building will be used for, and his descriptions paint a vivid picture of a state-of-the-art facility. "We have lost the infrastructure for our industry. I have a terrible time getting things done when they have to be outsourced, so that's why I'm making this mill as vertical as possible, because I'm sick of waiting for someone else to do it."

Once Cestari has a top-of-the-line mill up and running, it will need wool to process. "I said to myself, I'm getting sick of going out west to buy wool," Francis confides. "It costs a lot of money to ship it east. I decided that I needed local wool, but there isn't any. So we came up with a program. I noticed that we have been losing sheep numbers for years. In 1953, we had 54 million sheep in this country —the second largest producer of wool and sheep in the world, second only to Australia. All around here were wool sheep. Now, we're down to 5.4 million sheep. We lost 50 million sheep! But lamb prices are really high and wool prices are going up and up. So the future for sheep is here."

Francis devised a program—almost like a franchise—to help "grow" new local sheep farms. "I sat down and put on several hats: the hat of a shepherd, the hat of a mill owner, and the hat of a textile person. All three have to make out in this deal. So I said, I'm going to pay all the sheep people $3 a pound for wool—ten times what the going price was. I'll keep the price the same, regardless of the market year to year. Then I said, I'll even buy your lambs. Sell me your lambs when they're 100 pounds or more, and I'll pay you $200, so long as you don't shear the lamb. But then I came up with another idea. I'm going to have a trade-in program for ewes and rams." Francis' herd is populated with Targhee, Columbia, and Ramboullet sheep, and his program is based on helping new shepherds be successful—by selling them healthy sheep that are proven breeders, by helping to teach them to care for the sheep, by setting up shearing stations and ensuring that they get good value for their wool, and by purchasing their lambs and "trading in" their rams and ewes, so that they can grow their flocks.

A Cestari brochure titled "Important Points in Raising Wool Breeds," begins with an introduction explaining that the information is "my opinions based upon raising sheep and goats for over 71 years, starting at age 10. I was always, and am to this day, open to ideas on

how to be a successful shepherd and textile manufacturer. Along the way, some of the ideas and practices were not successful, but I learned from those mistakes and they caused me to be a better business person. So let's begin!" In discussing all of the components of his program, Francis explains, "I want to keep their costs low, and I want them to make money." The program is titled "Let's Grow Sheep Together!" and is set out in detail on the Cestari website.

As if this isn't enough, Francis has other ideas in the works, too. He travels all around the country, meeting with local yarn stores for "shepherd's day at the shop." This gives him a chance to talk to people about his yarn. "We establish a connection between the shepherd and the people who use our yarn. It's a wonderful relationship and I enjoy it, I really do. I tell shop owners that for every $10 they spend with me, I can put two blocks up [in the new mill], and we're building our mill block by block. We're creating excitement, and that's what really sells." Francis is also working with local universities to try to get linen raised domestically, and he guest teaches at the university's fashion school, and is even working with Virginia Commonwealth University to establish an internship program for future designers to see first-hand where the materials they work with come from and how they're developed. And, of particular interest to

Cestari Seminar Program

* Three days of lodging and breakfast in the Stonewall Jackson Hotel in Staunton, Virginia
* Three days of visits to Cestari mill and lunch in the cafe
* Two four-hour programs with knitting, crocheting, spinning, felting, dyeing, or weaving experts
* Performance at the American Shakespeare Theater in Staunton
* A visit to the Frontier Culture Museum's special textile program
* A ride on the Cestari Conastga wagon to sheep and lambing barns

"This will be a most educational and enjoyable event, and all of these early funds will go toward the construction of our new mill!"

me is Francis' three-day seminars for knitters, crocheters, and spinners (see inset box).

Francis tours me around his farm, nestled in the Shenandoah Valley at the foot of the Allegheny Mountains. We slip into the lambing barn, where some of the lambs are so newly born that they're only hours old. We inhale the smell of hay and the sense of peace, and admire the sun shining through the lambs' big ears, making them glow pink. In order to protect his flock from predators, Francis brings them into the corral in the evenings. "I'm having a sign made that reads, 'We count our sheep and our blessings every night,'" he laughs. I can't imagine a more beautiful or bucolic place for a shepherd to count his blessings than the Cestari farm. ⌘

Stacks of law books (below) attest to Francis Chester's long career as an attorney, as well as a life-long shepherd.

Cestari Sheep & Wool Company

Shepherd: Francis Chester

Website: cestarisheep.com

Products: Wool, cotton, and natural fiber blend yarns; shoes and slippers; accessories; sheepskins; home decor and vehicle accessories; knitting and crochet supplies

Programs: Let's Grow Sheep Together, Support the Mill, Cestari Seminar Program

23

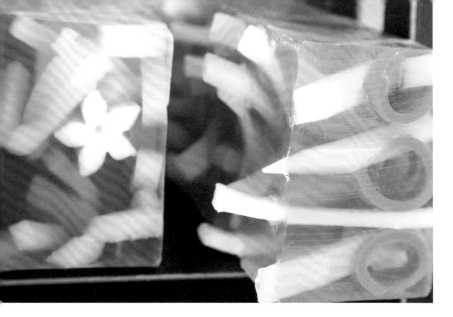

Soapmaking: Essential Journeys

After college graduation, Kimberly Masters and a friend rode their bicycles across the United States, camping along the way. "If tomatoes fell off the back of a truck, we'd have tomato soup for dinner," she laughs. With a cross-country tour under her belt, she took a job in Alaska guiding bicycle tours, and worked summers there for the next five years. When Kimberly left Alaska to guide in the lower 48 states for Woman Tours, she moved to Asheville and, during breaks between bicycle tours, she worked for a local outdoor school, leading students on backpacking trips and traveling around the country on recruiting trips.

During downtimes between bicycle trips, Kimberly began making soap for herself. "I love doing my own thing, and I love art—bookbinding, ceramics, tons of knitting, playing with murals. I wondered if I could make soap and sell it, as a way to make money and invest in the community here, and still have the time for travel." She began the Essential Journeys soap making business in 2004, attending trade shows and building up wholesale accounts, and fifteen years later, the business is thriving in a recently built studio added as part of her home renovation. In addition to soap making, Kimberly's ongoing employment with Woman Tours continues to take her all over the United States and the world.

The soap making process begins by heating glycerin and vegetable oils in large cookers. The substance is clear at this point, so the next step is to add natural pigments. Next, Kimberly uses molds to make the pieces that will go inside the soap and create any one of a number of designs. After the design

pieces are laid out in large bread pans, coloring and scent are added and the liquid is poured into the bread pans on top of the design pieces. When the soap hardens, it's popped out of the bread pans and typically sliced into individual bars. Kimberly loves finding "a synergy between color, scent, and design," and says that there are endless combinations and always a new way to bring innovative ideas to the process. As an added benefit, there is no waste; any leftover soap is simply grated up and can be melted down and used again. Even the boxes and packaging materials used to mail Essential Journeys products are largely reused and repurposed from other sources.

"I like the creativity of it every day—we have some basic patterns, we come up with new ideas all of the time, and we do all sorts of custom orders. It is so much more than just a chemistry project," Kimberly reflects. In addition to soaps, Essential Journeys now

carries lotions, arnica salve, beeswax-based lip balms, beer and honey soaps, and goats milk products. And the company just launched a new lotion—Artistic Journey—with labels that showcase the paintings of local artists.

Although her travels and work as a bicycle guide often take her away from home, Kimberly's home base is a lovely bungalow in Asheville, chock-full of artistic pieces collected from around the world, her own murals and artistic pursuits, and her mother's beautifully illustrated botanical paintings. She has created a strong network of creative connections in the town, and loves Asheville for its livability, the small independent businesses that populate its downtown, the numerous artists who make their homes in and around the River Arts District, and the 44 breweries that call Asheville home. She has found and nurtured an artistic pursuit that both fulfills her need for a creative outlet, and operates as a successful business that allows her the flexibility to continue pursuing her love of travel and of seeing the world from the seat of a bicycle. ⌘

Essential Journeys

Soapmaker: Kimberly Masters

Website: essentialjourneys.com

Instagram: essentialjourneys

Products: Soaps of all kinds, salves and butters, lip balm, bath salts, goats milk lotion and soap, craft beers soap, pottery, candles

Previous page: Spring is coming to the Smoky Mountains, viewed from the Blue Ridge Parkway near Asheville.
Above and below: Murals decorate the warehouses of Asheville's River Arts District.

Locally Produced: Echoview Fiber Mill

Every aspect of Echoview Fiber Mill reflects its commitment to sustainability and support of the local farming and fiber communities. "An innovative, state-of-the art fiber processing and manufacturing hub that is a catalyst for connecting community with commerce," reads one of its brochures. The mill, which opened in 2012, is Gold LEED certified and is housed in a building designed with low impact materials, light harvesting windows, solar panels, and even a charging station for electric vehicles. The lofty ceilings and light-filled interior create a feeling of spaciousness, and large glass second story windows welcome visitors to observe the milling machinery at work on the floor below. Even the walls of the facility are beautifully decorated with fiber-related artwork—some from local artisans, and some collected by owner and founder Julie Jensen during her travels around the world.

Echoview both produces and supplies farm and fiber goods. On the production side, the mill initially began by milling yarn for farmers who brought in a minimum of five pounds of fiber. However, economies of scale made this business model unsustainable, and the mill transitioned to purchasing batches of fiber from local farmers, and then milling the yarn and selling it under the Echoview label. The mill processes alpaca, mohair, angora, and many varieties of wool fibers that it purchases either from local farmers or from a large domestic fiber pool. Creative Director Grace Casey-Gouin walks us through each step of the process: cleaning and skirting, scouring and drying, fluffing, carding, pin drafting, and plying. The finished yarns are either sold "naked" to dyers, or are sold as Echoview yarns. Many of the mill's yarns

are dyed with natural dyes, and much of the alpaca yarn isn't dyed at all, but instead showcases the beauty and range of its natural colors. Echoview makes many related products, as well; for instance, its knitting machine produces soft and beautiful organic cotton blankets in a variety of sizes, and its wet felting machine creates products such as felted wool used by a cobbler for the insoles of shoes.

Across the street is a 78-acre working farm that Julie purchased in 2005, where alpacas, honeybees, and hops are raised with sustainable farming practices. Julie, a tax attorney from Washington, D.C., moved to western North Carolina after "accidentally falling in love with a small farm on a visit to Asheville," according to the Echoview website. She quickly became aware of the need for a small-batch, artisan mill, and the intersection between the local textile and farming industries. Her commitment to farming, environmental sustainability, and community led to the building and formation of Echoview. The farm's products, including Appalachian honey, grits, and sorghum molasses, are also sold under the Echoview

label. All of these products can be found on Echoview's website, along with a wide variety of knitted clothing, accessories, jewelry, and home decor. Echoview also produces and sells several lines of yarn, including botanically dyed worsted weight merino, naturally colored 100% alpaca yarn sourced from small, independent alpaca farms around the country, and a two-ply aran weight alpaca and merino blend in gorgeous tones of ivory, wheat, walnut, and ember. Echoview prides itself on products that are beautifully designed, of exceptional quality, and are described as "both simple and modern."

Echoview creates community as an invaluable end-point for small fiber farms in the area, but it pursues many other initiatives for community-oriented activities, as well. The spacious rooms in the building provide space for meetings, classes, and gatherings. Trunk shows and demonstrations are hosted, as well as events that draw residents together such as clothing swaps and seed trades. Natural dye demonstrations and classes are offered in the space, as well, and a community dye garden is in development. As its website states, "we embrace an age where community means something deeply local while also involving people all over the globe who share an interest and passion for the beauty of handmade things." ⌘

Echoview Fiber Mill

Website: echoviewnc.com

Address: 79 Jupiter Rd, Weaverville, N.C.

Phone: 855.693.4237

Products: Yarn, tools and dyes, clothing, accessories, jewelry, home decor, baby gifts, Echoview Farm products, workshops and classes

Allegheny
Pullover Hoodie by Andrea Hungerford

I love a hoodie with a flattering fit so that it looks nice enough to wear just about anywhere and is comfortable without being too slouchy. Cestari's Ashlawn beautifully blends cotton and wool for a wonderful three-season knit, and the unique construction let me create vertical stripes with Junkyarn speckles for a splash of color, reminiscent of a Baja beach hoodie.

SIZES
XS (S, M, L, XL, 2XL)
Shown in size M (intended to be worn with 4-6" of ease)

FINISHED MEASUREMENTS
Bust circumference 35.5 (39, 42.5, 47, 50.5, 55)"
Length from back neck 25 (25.5, 26, 27, 27.5, 28)"

MATERIALS
MC: Cestari Ash Lawn Collection 3 Ply DK weight (75% cotton/25% wool, 250 yds per 100 g), 5 (5, 6, 6, 7, 8) skeins in Natural White, or approximately 1040 (1165, 1295, 1460, 1595, 1770) yards

CC: Junkyarn Boss Sock 2-ply (80% superwash merino / 20% nylon, 400 yds per 100g), 2 (2, 2, 2, 2, 3) skeins in Laurie, or approximately 490 (545, 605, 685, 750, 830) yards

US 6 (4 mm) 24" circular needle
Tapestry needle, stitch marker, removable markers, spare knitting needle for three-needle BO, safety pin

GAUGE
19 sts and 28 rows = 4" in stripe pattern with 1 strand of MC and 2 strands of CC, blocked

NOTES
Front and back are knit flat from side to side. After sewing the shoulder seams, stitches are picked up from the armhole for the sleeves, which are knit flat to the wrist. Hood is picked up and knit from the neck edge. A circular needle is required to work the hood.

Always use MC single-stranded and CC double-stranded.

Where two options are given for an increase or decrease ("m1 or m1p," "k2tog or p2tog," "ssk or ssp"), use the knit increase/decrease on knit rows and the purl increase/decrease on purl rows.

STRIPE PATTERN
Stripe pattern repeats over 30 rows. Odd-numbered rows are WS, even-numbered rows are RS.

Rows 1-16: With MC and beg with a purl row (WS), work 16 rows stockinette.
Row 17 (WS): With CC held double, knit.
Rows 18-21: With MC and beg with a knit row (RS), work 4 rows stockinette.
Rows 22-25: With CC held double and beg with a knit row (RS), work 4 rows stockinette.
Rows 26-29: With MC and beg with a knit row (RS), work 4 rows stockinette.
Row 30 (RS): With CC held double, purl.

MC should be joined before Rows 1 and 18 and cut after Rows 16 and 29; otherwise, carry it up the side of the work when not in use. CC should be joined before Row 17 and cut after Row 30; otherwise, carry it up the side of the work when not in use.

DIRECTIONS
BACK
With CC (MC, MC, MC, MC, MC), CO 121 (124, 126, 128, 131, 133) sts. Work in stripe patt beginning with Row 22 (16, 10, 2, 26, 18) (RS).

Shape Right Shoulder:
Work 8 (8, 8, 8, 6, 8) rows even, ending with a WS row.
Inc Row (RS): Work 2 sts, m1 or m1p (see Notes), work to end. 1 st inc'd.
Repeat Inc Row on every 6 (6, 8, 6, 8, 8)th row 4 (4, 4, 6, 6, 6) more times. 126 (129, 131, 135, 138, 140) sts.
Work 5 (9, 7, 9, 5, 9) rows even, ending with a WS row.

With RS facing, place a removable marker in the right-hand edge of the work for end of shoulder.

Back Neck:
Work 48 (52, 52, 56, 56, 60) rows even, ending with a WS row.
Shape Left Shoulder:
With RS facing, place a removable marker in the right-hand edge of the work for beginning of shoulder.

Work 6 (10, 8, 10, 6, 10) rows even, ending with a WS row.
Dec Row (RS): Work 2 sts, ssk or ssp (see Notes), work to end. 1 st dec'd.
Rep Dec Row on every 6 (6, 8, 6, 8, 8)th row 4 (4, 4, 6, 6, 6) more times. 121 (124, 126, 128, 131, 133) sts rem.
Work 7 (7, 7, 7, 5, 7) rows even, ending with Row 25 (1, 7, 15, 21, 29) of stripe patt.
BO all sts.

FRONT
With CC (MC, MC, MC, MC, MC), CO 121 (124, 126, 128, 131, 133) sts. Work in stripe patt beginning with Row 22 (16, 10, 2, 26, 18) (RS).

Shape Left Shoulder:
Work 8 (8, 8, 8, 6, 8) rows even, ending with a WS row.
Inc Row (RS): Work 2 sts, m1 or m1p, work to end. 1 st inc'd.
Repeat Inc Row on every 6 (6, 8, 6, 8, 8)th row 4 (4, 4, 6, 6, 6) more times. 126 (129, 131, 135, 138, 140) sts.
Work 5 (9, 7, 9, 5, 9) rows even, ending with a WS row.

Front Neck:
BO 2 sts at beg of next 12 (13, 13, 14, 14, 15) RS rows. 102 (103, 105, 107, 110, 110) sts rem. Last row worked should be Row 22 of stripe patt.
Work 2 rows even, ending with a RS row.
Use the backward loop method to CO 2 sts at end of next 12 (13, 13, 14, 14, 15) WS rows. 126 (129, 131, 135, 138, 140) sts.

Shape Right Shoulder:
Work 6 (10, 8, 10, 6, 10) rows even, ending with a WS row.
Dec row (RS): Work 2 sts, ssk or ssp, work to end. 1 st dec'd.
Rep dec row on every 6 (6, 8, 6, 8, 8)th row 4 (4, 4, 6, 6, 6) more times. 121 (124, 126, 128, 131, 133) sts rem.
Work 7 (7, 7, 7, 5, 7) rows even, ending with Row 25 (1, 7, 15, 21, 29) of stripe patt.
BO all sts.

SLEEVES
Block back and front to schematic measurements. Sew shoulder seams, matching markers on back to neck edges on front.

Mark 7 (7.5, 8, 8.5, 9, 9.5)" to either side of shoulder seam. With RS facing and using MC (MC, MC, MC, CC, MC), pick up and knit 66 (71, 76, 81, 85, 90) sts between the markers.

Work in stripe patt beg with Row 27 (3, 9, 17, 23, 1) (WS). Work 7 (7, 7, 5, 5, 5) rows even, ending with a WS row.

Dec Row (RS): Work 2 sts, ssk or ssp, work to last 4 sts, k2tog or p2tog, work 2 sts. 2 sts dec'd. Repeat Dec Row on every 10 (8, 8, 6, 6, 6)th row 9 (4, 9, 4, 4, 12) more times, then on every 12 (10, 10, 8, 8, 8)th row 1 (7, 3, 10, 10, 4) time(s). 44 (47, 50, 51, 55, 56) sts rem. Sleeve measures about 15.75" from pick-up row.

Work even until sleeve measures 17.5" from pick-up row, or desired length. BO all sts.

HOOD
With RS facing, using MC and the backward loop method CO 5 sts on right needle, then beginning at base of V-neck, pick up and knit 24 (26, 26, 28, 28, 30) sts up front neck edge, 34 (36, 36, 38, 38, 40) sts across back neck, and 24 (26, 26, 28, 28, 30) sts down opposite front neck edge. At end, backward loop CO 5 sts. 92 (98, 98, 104, 104, 110) sts.

Work in stripe patt beginning with Row 1 (WS).

Work even until hood measures 11.5 (12, 12, 12.5, 12.5, 13)", ending with a WS row. Place a marker in the center of the row.

Shape Top:
Dec Row (RS): Work in established pattern to 3 sts before m, k2tog or p2tog, work 1, sl marker, work 1, ssk or ssp, work to end. 2 sts dec'd. Repeat Dec Row on every RS row 5 more times. 80 (86, 86, 92, 92, 98) sts rem.
Work 1 WS row even.

Divide sts in half. With right sides facing, join the two halves with a three-needle BO.

FINISHING
Fold the extra 5 sts at each end of hood to the inside and using MC threaded on a tapestry needle, slip

stitch the long edge in place to make the drawstring casing, leaving the short ends open. Using 2 strands of CC, CO 2 sts. *K2, do not turn. Slip sts from right needle tip to left and draw yarn snugly across back of work. Repeat from * until cord measures about 45", or desired length. BO and weave in ends. Use a safety pin to run the drawstring through the casing, then knot each end to prevent the string from being pulled out.

Sew side and sleeve seams. Fold lower 1.5" of body to WS and slip stitch in place for hem.
Weave in ends. Block.

TECHNIQUES
Three-Needle Bind Off
Have the two pieces to be joined on separate needles held together in the left hand. Using a third needle, insert into first st on front needle, then first st on back needle and knit them together. *Insert into next st on front needle, then next st on back needle and knit them together, then pass first st on right needle over second to BO 1 st. Repeat from *.

ABBREVIATIONS
BO   bind off
CC   contrast color
CO   cast on
dec(s/'d)   decrease(s)/decreased

inc(s/'d)   increase(s)/increased

k   knit

k2tog   knit 2 together

m1   make 1: with right needle, pick up running thread between needles from back to front and place it on left needle, then knit it through the back loop

m1P   make 1 purl: with right needle, pick up running thread between needles from front to back, place on left needle, purl it through the front loop.

MC   main color

p   purl

p2tog   purl 2 together

patt   pattern

pm   place marker

rem   remain(s)

rep   repeat

RS   right side

sl   slip

ssk   [slip 1 as if to knit] 2 times, insert left needle into fronts of these sts and knit them together

St st   stockinette stitch

st(s)   stitch(es)

WS   wrong side

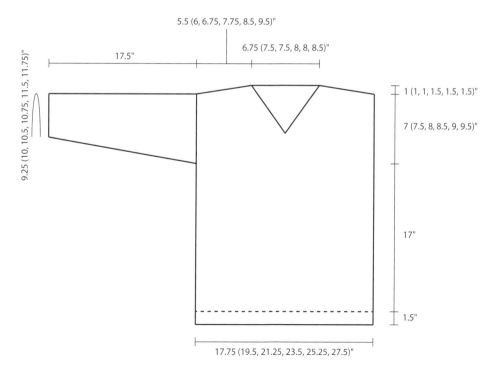

5.5 (6, 6.75, 7.75, 8.5, 9.5)"

6.75 (7.5, 7.5, 8, 8, 8.5)"

17.5"

9.25 (10, 10.5, 10.75, 11.5, 11.75)"

1 (1, 1, 1.5, 1.5, 1.5)"

7 (7.5, 8, 8.5, 9, 9.5)"

17"

1.5"

17.75 (19.5, 21.25, 23.5, 25.25, 27.5)"

Hand-Dyed Speckles: Junkyarn

Kemper Wray was an artist long before she began dyeing yarn. With a background in art history and an MFA in creative writing, she has been immersed in the creative process much of her life. But it was her love for color that drew her to yarn dyeing. "It's like pouring and painting layers of color," she explains. Junkyarns showcase this love of color in their brilliant, sometimes unexpected combinations, their bright speckled pops, and their deeply saturated hues. Kemper's entire dyeing process is an expression of creativity. The colors come from patterns of pouring on color, or the movement of the water as the yarns "cook." Speckles are introduced by putting on a dry power and then introducing steam. Changing the process can alter the results, too. "Sometimes I'll introduce heat in the oven—I'll pour on the color in a couple of different spots in a way that lets the colors blend together, then I'll put a speckle on top, then the heat from the oven sets the speckle." After heat setting the color, Kemper uses a bath of textile detergent to wash away any remaining particles of dye, then a lanolin wash to bring back softness to the yarn.

The one-of-a-kind colors are not the only thing unique about Junkyarn, though. All of the colorways are named for women whose creativity or activism is inspiring to Kemper. "There's so many amazing women out there who inspire me," she says, "and now especially, women need to help women. I think supporting all women and female identifying people is important, and I think it doesn't matter where they're from or what they look like." Kemper puts a great deal of time into researching women who have been influential in all different cultures and communities. Most of the time, she begins her creative process with an inspiring woman, and aspects of that woman's life or achievements help her "realize" the color. For instance, one of her newest colorways, inspired by Indira Gandhi, has a golden yellow base reminiscent of turmeric, and speckled pops like spices scattered over the top. It is a color that evokes the "feeling" of India and perfectly reflects the woman for whom it is named.

One of the aspects of her business that Kemper most likes is collaborating with local yarn stores, helping to match her colorways and bases with what a particular LYS' customers will like. "I love to work with the shop owners to learn what their customers like before I send them colors, and I always offer to help pick out colors. It depends on what types of garments their customers are knitting, and what colors they gravitate to." Kemper also dyes custom colors for shops—like Beverly Cleary for Portland's Starlight Knitting Society, named for a well-known children's author who lived and wrote there.

In addition to wholesaling yarn to local yarn stores, Kemper sells through her own store online, at shows like Vogue Knitting Live and Stitches West, and at LYS trunk shows. She loves to collaborate with other people, including shop owners and designers, and values the opportunity that traveling to shows gives her to meet people. "Sometimes I like to step back and let people pick their own colors at shows," she says, "and sometimes I like to make suggestions about how to put colors together. It's exciting to help people stretch themselves and look at color in a different way. You can have fun with it without any real risk. The only risk is trying something crazy that you won't like and you'll have to undo it. You just need to loosen up about it!" ⌘

One of the many squirrel figurines—this one a gift, purchased from a flea market in Germany—that line Kemper's mantel and the transom above a doorway, in homage to her childhood nickname "squirrel" (above).

Andrea Mowry's Comfort Fade Cardi beautifully showcases Junkyarn colors Fleur, Dolly, Diana, and Lara (left).

Junkyarn

Yarn Dyer and Color Creator: Kemper Wray

Website: junkyarn.com

Instagram: wraybot

Products: In-stock and dyed-to-order yarns and kits, in a variety of bases and ever-changing colorways

The Kemper Wrap
by Mara Catherine Bryner

FINISHED MEASUREMENTS
24" tall and 64" wide

MATERIALS
Junkyarn Smooth Sock (75% superwash merino/25% nylon, 463 yards per 100 g)
A: 1 skein in Indira (yellow)
B: 1 skein in Hermione (pink)
C: 1 skein in Virginia (dark gray)

Junkyarn Lavish Lace (70% kid mohair/30% silk, 435 yards per 100 g)
D: 1 skein in Hermione (pink)

US 6 (4 mm) circular needle, 32" or longer
Stitch holder or waste yarn, stitch marker, tapestry needle, blocking wires (optional)

GAUGE
22 stitches and 28 rows = 4" in pattern with Smooth Sock held double, blocked

Gauge is not crucial for this design, but if your gauge is significantly different your wrap
will be a different size than stated, and you may require more or less yarn.

NOTES

Kemper is knit from the center out, on the bias. The center triangle is knit first, then each side triangle is worked separately.

A slipped-stitch edging is worked on the long edges of the wrap. Take care to keep the edging tension loose to match the stretch of the bias fabric.

Smooth Sock is used double-stranded throughout, sometimes as two strands of the same color and sometimes as one strand each of two colors. We recommend winding each skein into two equal-sized balls before beginning. Lavish Lace is used alone, single-stranded, on every 7th and 8th row throughout most of shawl.

When changing between Smooth Sock and Lavish Lace, don't cut the yarn(s) not in use. Carry the unused strand(s) loosely up the work inside the slipped-stitch edging.

SPECIAL STITCHES

[K1, yo, k1]: Remove marker, knit next st but do not drop from left needle, replace marker on right needle, yo, knit into same stitch again and drop original stitch from left needle. (2 sts inc'd in 1 st)
KSK (slipped-stitch edge treatment for RS rows): K1, sl 1 purlwise with yarn in front (pwise wyif), k1.
SKS (slipped-stitch edge treatment for WS rows): Sl 1 pwise wyif, k1, sl 1 pwise wyif.

PATTERN
CENTER TRIANGLE

Setup Section:
With 2 strands of A held together, use the long-tail method to CO 9 sts.
Row 1 (WS): SKS (see Special Stitches), k1, p1, pm, k1, SKS.
Row 2 (RS): KSK (see Special Stitches), k1, [k1, yo, k1] (see Special Stitches), k1, KSK. 11 sts.
Row 3: SKS, k2, p1, sl m, k2, SKS.
Row 4: KSK, kfb, knit to marker, [k1, yo, k1], knit to last 4 sts, kfb, KSK. 4 sts inc'd
Row 5: SKS, knit to 1 st before marker, p1, sl m, knit to last 3 sts, SKS.
Rows 6 & 7: Repeat Rows 4 & 5. 19 sts.
Join in a single strand of Lavish Lace (yarn D).
Row 8 (laceweight row): With D, KSK, kfb, knit to marker, [k1, yo, k1], knit to last 4 sts, kfb, KSK. 23 sts.
Row 9 (laceweight row): With D, SKS, *k2tog, yo; rep from * to 1 st before marker, p1, sl m, **yo, ssk; rep from ** to last 3 sts, SKS.

Main Triangle:

Continue with 2 strands of A.

Row 1 (RS): With 2 strands of Smooth Sock, KSK, kfb, knit to marker, [k1, yo, k1], knit to last 4 sts, kfb, KSK. 4 sts inc'd.

Row 2 (WS): With 2 strands of Smooth Sock, SKS, knit to 1 st before marker, p1, sl m, knit to last 3 sts, SKS.

Rows 3–6: Repeat Rows 1 & 2 two times.

Row 7 (laceweight row): With D, KSK, kfb, knit to marker, [k1, yo, k1], knit to last 4 sts, kfb, KSK. 4 sts inc'd.

Row 8 (laceweight row): With D, SKS, *k2tog, yo; rep from * to 1 st before marker, p1, sl m, **yo, ssk; rep from ** to last 3 sts, SKS.

Continuing with 2 strands of A, repeat Rows 1–8 seven more times. 151 sts. Cut 1 strand of A and join in 1 strand of B.

With 1 strand each of A + B held together, repeat Rows 1–8 two times, then Rows 1–6 only once. 195 sts.

Divide Stitches:

Note: You will keep the first 97 stitches plus half of the center stitch on the needle for Side A, and transfer the other half of the center stitch and the remaining 97 stitches to a holder or waste yarn to wait for Side B.

With RS facing, beginning at left-hand edge of piece and working left to right, slip 97 sts plus the left leg of the center st to a holder or waste yarn. 97 sts + the right leg of center st remain on needle. You will treat each half of the center st as its own stitch from now on, making 98 effective sts currently on the needle.

SIDE A

Section 1:

Continue with 1 strand each of A + B held together.

Row 1 (RS, laceweight row): With D, KSK, kfb, knit to last 5 sts, k2tog, KSK.

Row 2 (WS, laceweight row): With D, SKS, purl to last 3 sts, SKS.

Row 3: With 2 strands of Smooth Sock, KSK, kfb, knit to last 5 sts, k2tog, KSK.

Row 4: With 2 strands of Smooth Sock, SKS, knit to last 3 sts, SKS.

Rows 5 & 6: Repeat Rows 3 & 4.

Continuing with 1 strand each of A + B, repeat Rows 1–6 three more times. Cut A and join in a second strand of B.

With 2 strands of B, repeat Rows 1–6 six times. Cut 1 strand of B and join in 1 strand of C.
With 1 strand each of B + C, repeat Rows 1–6 five times, then repeat Rows 1 & 2 only once.

Section II:
Note: In this section, you will decrease at both edges of the work to shape the wrap into a rectangle.
Cut B and join in a second strand of C.
Row 1 (RS): With 2 strands of Smooth Sock, KSK, ssk, knit to last 5 stitches, k2tog, KSK. 2 sts dec'd.
Row 2 (WS): With 2 strands of Smooth Sock, SKS, knit to last 3 sts, SKS.
Rows 3–6: Repeat Rows 1 & 2 two times.
Row 7 (laceweight row): With D, KSK, ssk, knit to last 5 stitches, k2tog, KSK. 2 sts dec'd.
Row 8 (laceweight row): With D, SKS, *k2tog, yo; rep from * to last 3 sts, SKS.

Continuing with 2 strands of C, repeat Rows 1–8 nine more times. 18 sts remain. Cut D; remainder of Side A is worked with C only.
Repeat Rows 1 & 2 five times. 8 sts remain.

Next Row (RS): KSK, k2tog, KSK. 7 sts.
Next Row (WS): SKS, k1, SKS.
Next Row: K1, sl 1 pwise wyif, sl 1, k2tog, psso, k1. 5 sts.
Next Row: Sl 1 pwise wyif, k3, sl 1 pwise wyif.
Next Row: K1, sl 1, k2tog, psso, k1. 3 sts.
Next Row: Sl 1, k2tog, psso. 1 st.
Break yarn and fasten off remaining st.

SIDE B
Section I:
Transfer the 98 sts (97 sts + half of center st) from holder to needle. Join a single strand of D with RS facing.
Row 1 (RS, laceweight row): With D, KSK, ssk, knit to last 4 sts, kfb, KSK.
Row 2 (WS, laceweight row): With D, SKS, purl to last 3 sts, SKS. Drop D.
Row 3: With 2 strands of Smooth Sock, KSK, ssk, knit to last 4 sts, kfb, KSK.
Row 4: With 2 strands of Smooth Sock, SKS, knit to last 3 sts, SKS.
Rows 5 & 6: Repeat Rows 3 & 4.
Continuing with 1 strand each of A and B, repeat Rows 1–6 three more times.
Change to 2 strands of B. Repeat Rows 1–6 six times.

Change to 1 strand of B and 1 strand of C. Repeat Rows 1–6 five times, then repeat Rows 1 & 2 only once.

Section II:
Work as for Side A Section II.

FINISHING
Weave in ends and block, using blocking wires if available to achieve a nicely shaped rectangle.

ABBREVIATIONS

BO – bind off   CO - cast on
Dec'd – decreased   Inc'd – increased
K – knit   Kfb – knit into front and back of same st
K2tog – knit 2 sts together   Rem – remain
Rep – repeat   P – purl
RS – right side   Sl – slip
Sl 1, k2tog, psso – slip 1 knitwise, knit 2 together, pass slipped st over the k2tog
Ssk – [slip 1 as if to knit] 2 times, insert left needle into fronts of these 2 sts and knit them together
St(s) – stitch(es)   WS – wrong side
Yo – yarn over

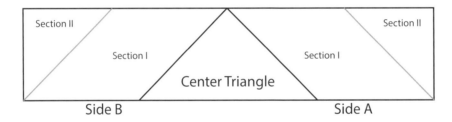

On the Loom: Toft Cottage Weavery

The first thing you notice when you enter Toft Cottage Weavery's cozy studio is the imposing structure of the antique barn loom. The loom, which is 200 - 250 years old, was found in the attic of an old house in Maine, and Patricia Rushmore purchased it in Vermont, where she attended classes at the Marshfield School of Weaving. The loom is held together with wooden pegs, and amazingly, it can be dissembled to a "pile of sticks" in about fifteen minutes. Patricia weaves wool rugs on the loom, but she tells me that it can do anything from heavy rug wool to fine linens. It is her favorite loom, she says, because "you climb in and sit in here, and you're in the world of weaving. It really takes you into a historic, traditional weaving environment."

Patricia learned to weave fifteen years ago, taking her first lessons from an 80-year-old gentleman while living in Pennsylvania. "After the first class, I knew this was for me," she recalls. After retirement, she began weaving full-time on multiple looms in her studio, as well as teaching others on two student looms. Former students also rent the looms and the space, which gives Patricia an opportunity to weave with others. "Weaving can be so solitary. Having others working here in the studio gives us a chance to share ideas, and weaving together creates community," she explains. Patricia is also active in the Handweavers Guild of the New River Valley, which gives her a forum to meet with other knitters, spinners, and weavers, and to learn new techniques from national instructors periodically sponsored by the guild.

Wool is one of Patricia's favorite fibers to work with, and unlike many other weavers, she incorporates a lot of knitting and novelty yarns as well, because she loves how it affects

the feel and look of the finished project. She gravitates toward using basic patterns, and then experimenting with many different fibers and color combinations. For instance, she shows me one exquisite shawl that was knit from 7-8 different yarns, including a bouclé yarn that gives it a unique and beautiful texture. In addition to working with a variety of yarns, Patricia has begun dyeing her own yarns and incorporating those into her weaving, and doing inlay work by hand while the weaving is on the loom. Many of her weavings are destined to become shawls, rugs, and wool throws. "I love shawls because they bring warmth and comfort, like a hug," she smiles.

Weaving is a multi-step process, and Patricia walks me through some of the basics. She first comes up with the design and the colors she'll use and puts it down on paper. Next, she shows me the large warping board and explains how she winds her yarns in the predetermined colors and patterns on the board. Then she brings the entire thing to the back of the loom to wind it on the back beam. Next steps include threading the heddles and hooking up the treadles (foot pedals) according to the pattern that Patricia has designed. Set-up is 50-60% of the work of weaving, Patricia explains. Just as important is the post-production work: wet-finishing the wool by washing, cleansing, and steaming the finished pieces, so that the wool blooms, much like wet-blocking a knitted piece.

Patricia sells most of her pieces at local shows and through custom work. She often announces a completed piece on Facebook and sells it almost immediately. She avoids any production-level or repetitive

work because she wants to continue to find the enjoyment and creativity that weaving brings her. And, while weaving can be backbreaking work, Patricia says that "I'm just at my happiest when I'm here weaving. You almost feel unsettled until you can get back to the loom—it's meditative. Just the whole act of creating something... I don't need to do this for a living, but I need it for my soul, so as long as I have the freedom to create, then I'm happy." ⌘

Toft Cottage Weavery

Textile artist and weaver:
Patricia Rushmore

Website:
toftcottageweavery.com

Facebook: Toft Cottage
Weavery

Studio: 8500 Callaway Rd.,
Callaway, Virginia

On Open Studio days in Asheville's River Arts District, visitors can stop in to get a glimpse of over 200 artists and their tools (like the paints palette, top left).

Artist Ka Amorastreya at work during a River Arts District Open Studio day (bottom left).

Knitwear Design: Appalachian Knits

Many knitwear designers begin their avocation by designing for themselves, in an attempt to create garments that best fit their bodies and their styles. Jennifer Sadler and Christina Danaee, the knitwear team of Appalachian Knits, began in this way and have continued to focus on fit and functionality. "I'm inspired by things that I would want in my wardrobe—functional, fun and comfortable," explains Jennifer. "I like garments without a lot of waist shaping because that's how I prefer to wear clothes—a little more oversized and comfortable—which I hope will encourage more people to knit them." Jennifer gravitates toward designing accessories, because "they don't have to fit or be sized, and they can fit a wide variety of body styles." Christina, on the other hand, has a background in dressmaking and loves sweater design. She loves the fit of raglan sweaters, and the rhythm of knitting in the round, and many of her pullover designs reflect this preference.

While both members of the design team say that rustic wools are closest to their hearts, they also enjoy experimenting with blends like silk and linen, or cotton and wool. "We try to design for all seasons," Christina says. The team's design process typically begins with the yarns they want to focus on. Christina says, "we're trying to focus on yarns that come from a certain area, to let people know about regional yarns. That's not something that designers have done in this area before. I think it's important to support the small farms, the people who are still making the land work the way it used to. Many small farms here have heritage breeds, and the fibers are something special that you can't get anywhere else." Jennifer adds that using local yarns "is a good reflection of where your heart is. I grew up here. This area is really important to both Christina and me, and we want to work with materials that are close to our hearts and support our community."

While there are many small alpaca farms in western North Carolina, and several well-established farms selling yarns created with their own fiber in the Asheville area, most don't have an online presence, which makes it difficult for most knitters find them. The Appalachian Knits team hopes to bring attention to the availability of unique yarns in the area, and ultimately help the farms get their products into the hands of knitters. Christina has begun teaching classes at Echoview Fiber Mill and helping the mill to spread the word about its own yarns, which in turn supports the small farms who sell their fleece to Echoview. "I want people to keep raising fiber animals here," she says.

The two friends, who initially met on Instagram and then in real life once they realized that they lived in the same town, draw encouragement and inspiration from each other. "I've enjoyed working with somebody else and getting their feedback," Jennifer smiles. "What's fun about working with Jennifer," Christina adds, "is that she makes some design decisions, and I make others, so in the end, our collection pieces complement and balance each other." ⌘

Appalachian Knits

Designers: Christina Danaee and Jennifer Sadler

Website: christinadanaee.com

Instagram: appalachianknits

Ravelry: xtinawithwolves and jaykayknits

Luminous Yarn Lights
by Andrea Hungerford

I have a craft room that is chock full of baskets of leftover yarn. Some of these are full skeins, but most are balls of yarn in varying sizes, all leftover from bygone knitting projects. I am always looking for uses for this yarn stash that is too pretty to throw away, but not enough remaining for another knitting project. I worry that if I don't put my leftovers to good use, someday I'll be buried in yarn!

This project is the perfect second life for yarn leftovers. I used speckled yarn for all of these yarn lights, but you could achieve a totally different effect with earthy, tweedy tones. Or how about using all white yarn to create globes that would look as if they were fairy lights when they glowed at night? If you have yarn from a gradient set, you could use all of the different colors from the gradient to create a beautiful tonal look. These globes are beautiful in their own right, but I especially like how they remind me of favorite projects or yarn acquired on trips and travels, every time I look up and see them glowing.

Supplies:
* Glue-All
* measuring cup, Tupperware tub, stick to stir
* black marking pen
* 8.5" – 10" playground ball
* pump to inflate and needle to deflate ball
* yarn (I used fingering weight, approx. 225 yds for 8.5" globe)
* plastic trash bags
* small bowl to balance ball on

Cut open plastic bag so it lays flat, and place it on your work surface. Pull a second bag over your head, cutting holes in the top and sides for arms and head. (You will get a lot of splattering from this project, and these plastic bags will help protect your clothes and make cleanup easier.)

1. Inflate ball.
2. Using black pen, mark a circle approx. 4" in diameter on bottom and approx. 1" in diameter on top (this is where you'll run the cord through and access the light fixture).

3. Pour ½ cup glue and ½ cup water into tub (this should be enough glue for one globe—you can use more glue, just always keep the glue to water ratio 1:1).
4. Stir well.
5. Wind yarn into a cake and place in tub of glue.
6. Taking the end of the yarn, start wrapping it— covered with glue—around the ball. It helps to hold the ball against your chest when you're wrapping or rotating it (which is why the plastic smock is essential). Wind in a criss-cross motion to start.
7. As you're winding, take special care to create a firm edge around the bottom opening, keeping it clear of any strands of yarn (if a few cross over, don't worry —you can push them back when you're done). Work to keep the smaller top hole open too, but this isn't essential, as you can push the yarn aside when you're done wrapping to expose this circle.

8. It isn't necessary to wind in any particular pattern or style. Just remember to try to fill in any gaping holes; keep the distribution as even as possible; create a firm edge around the larger bottom circle; and don't let the strands cross the bottom circle.

57

9. Wrap until you run out of yarn, or until you feel that your strands are dense enough. Cut yarn and tuck loose end under strands of yarn to secure.

10. Check the two circles you drew. Push away any strands of yarn to keep these spaces clear.

10. Place yarn on bowl (sides of bowl shouldn't touch wet yarn, but should only touch the wider circle you drew at the bottom). Pour remaining glue mixture over the top and sides of the ball.

11. Let dry completely (takes about two days).

12. Using pump needle, deflate ball. Gently pull it away from sides of yarn globe and extract out of the larger bottom opening.

13. Thread the cord in from the bottom of the globe, up through the small opening in the top. The top of the socket should rest against this opening, holding the light fixture in place inside the globe. If desired, you can wrap white electrical tape around the top of the socket to create a larger "plug".

14. Use cloth, ribbon, or material of your choice to wind around the cord to create a decorative finish.

15. Hang your globe, screw in lightbulb, plug into wall socket, and enjoy! ⌘

58

Signs of spring in and around Asheville.

Woodworking: Ray Jones Woodcrafts

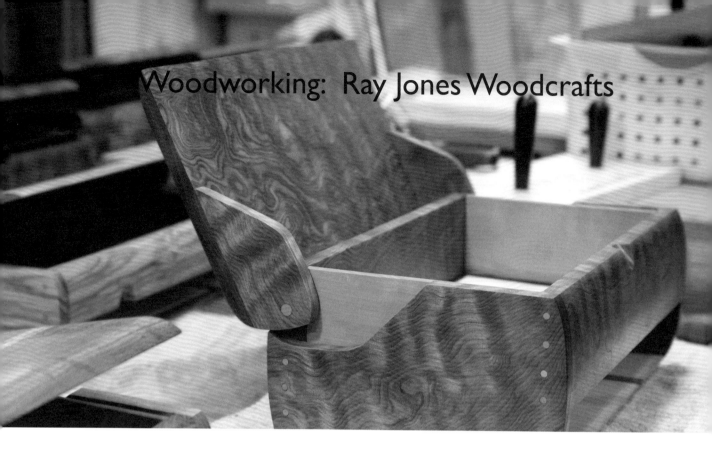

You can see evidence of Ray Jones' engineering background and his decades of experience with woodworking in the fine details and careful construction of his wooden boxes. While Ray studied aeronautical engineering in college, he credits the construction work he did during high school and college summers as "one of those life-changing experiences" that inspired him to begin woodworking. "The man I worked for was a great guy, he loved to teach, and to him, it was more important to do it right than to do it fast. He gave me a lot of confidence working with my hands. When I graduated from college, I moved to Los Angeles, rented a house, and instead of buying furniture, I bought tools and started making my own furniture." Ray didn't continue making furniture—the last piece he made was a rocking chair for his wife Linda when she was pregnant with their twin sons, sized to her exact measurements —but he began making boxes. In fact, the boxes he still makes today are based on a design he created for Linda many years ago.

Ray eventually left his engineering job to focus on woodworking, and he and his family moved to Asheville because of the strong crafts community and the opportunity to be within driving distance of family. For 36 years, he's built boxes full-time, and is still inspired by the process. "I love wood. A piece of wood is beautiful just on its own, so you're starting with a material that is already beautiful and, under the right conditions, renewable." One of the hallmarks of Ray's work is the number of different types of wood he uses—everything from Bird's Eye Maple to Purple Heart, from Curly Redwood to Africa Bubinga. One of his favorite woods to work with is Koa, from Hawaii, because it has warm color and often has a lot of depth. He loves woods with "lots of figure," meaning burls or curls in the grain. Every bit of Ray's boxes are constructed from wood, including the hinges and the dowels that hold them together, except for the velvet lining.

At a rate of about 400 boxes a year, Ray tells me that over the years, he's made 14,000 boxes. They come in a variety of sizes, and inside are cleverly constructed dividers that fit jewelry, a collection of watches, an assortment of writing pens, or a selection of teas. The dividers are removable, so that the box can be used to hold anything its owner desires. "Everybody can use a box," Ray smiles. "They work well for both men and women, and it can be difficult to find gifts for men—particularly handmade gifts at craft shows." But boxes make the best gifts, because they are the ultimate functional art. The recipient can always find a purpose that will be both personal and useful. Ray also constructs intricate, one-of-a-kind speciality boxes in unusual geometric shapes, that fit together ingeniously and always produce oohs and ahhs when he opens them up at craft shows. Some of these he calls "halfmoon" boxes because when viewed from the side, they are almost semicircular. The drawers are individually shaped to fit the contours of the box body, and even the drawer pulls are carved from wood.

Ray's custom work has produced a variety of unusual projects, including a box for a burial urn, ping pong paddles and a case that President Bush gifted to the Chinese government at the Beijing Olympics, and once, long ago in Los Angeles, a business card holder that a woman asked Ray to make to match her bed. Most of Ray's work is sold at juried craft shows—he travels extensively and typically sells at about 12 shows a year—and through his website, as well as at a few select galleries. Often, Ray's wife Linda accompanies him, and she has begun using the small pieces left over from his work to create woodturned pens. Linda's pens—which have unique embellishments that create all different kinds of character, from steampunk to fairy dust glitter—are sold under her own moniker, Dancing Spiral Woodturning.

Regardless of whether the box is simple and elegant, or as complex as a puzzle box, Ray explains that "all of my boxes are meant to be used, and people can see that. They're meant to be handled and touched. I try to make them feel as good as they look. I don't use any stains, because there are so many natural colors that it's hard to improve on Mother Nature." ⌘

Ray Jones Woodcrafts

Designer/Craftsman: Ray Jones

Website: rayjoneswoodboxes.com

Products: Small, medium, and large conventional boxes, pen boxes, and specialty boxes

Dancing Spiral Woodturning

Designer/Craftswoman: Linda Hynson

Website: dswoodturning.com

Products: Pens, pencils, styluses, seam rippers and other accessories

63

Murals can be found all around Asheville, including under freeway overpasses (middle), and even in the White Duck Taco Shop (bottom).

Sewing: Vesta Patterns

When you're traveling around the world, from Indonesia to China to Turkey and everywhere in between, and all of your possessions fit into one backpack, you need clothes that are versatile. It was during this time that Whitney Hills discovered her love of merino wool. "It worked in the hot and the cold, it wicked away sweat, it dried quickly—it was like magic!" she recalls. But once she stopped traveling and was ready to rebuild her wardrobe, she couldn't find any pieces that fit her well and didn't almost immediately fall apart. "I was tired of looking at myself and my body through the lens of ready-made fashion. When something doesn't fit, instead of thinking, 'this item doesn't fit me,' we default to 'I don't fit this.' It began to make me feel like I didn't fit in anywhere."

A growing awareness of the ecological and social damage caused by "fast fashion" inspired Whitney to explore creating clothing for herself, and after one sewing class, she was sold. "Two pieces of cloth, sewn together, and you have a garment!" she laughs. The sewing patterns available at that time didn't give her the results she was looking for, though, so she began to teach herself how to draft patterns. Drawing inspiration from Natalie Chanin's work, Whitney began to intensively study what made garments fit well. "I sewed t-shirt after t-shirt, six hours a day, and I spent over a year experimenting with different necklines and shoulder shaping."

The result was the first Vesta pattern: the Grail, a simple knit top with multiple sleeve lengths. It is really three different patterns for the same basic garment piece, to give makers a choice of shaping, depending on their own body style. "I hate all of the 'dress to flatter yourself' talk," explains Whitney. "You always hear 'minimize your problem areas.' All that language is about something being wrong with you, so here, let our clothing 'fix' you." Instead, Whitney loves the idea of

engaging with clothing as costume—as an opportunity to try out different personas, and even as self-therapy and self-exploration. After teaching herself to sew and to draft patterns, Whitney embarked on learning all of the skills necessary to create a published pattern: she learned how to work with CAD software, she studied how to fine-tune grading the patterns, she worked with one of only two tissue paper printers in North America to generate the printed patterns, and she designed all of the pattern packaging. "Every step of making a pattern is an art," she explains. "I wanted to take what can be a very complex, three-dimensional concept and explain it in a simple way that isn't intimidating to a beginner." After the Grail pattern, she switched to digital production, and designed the Fable dress pattern.

Whitney is no stranger to stepping outside of her comfort zone; home schooled as a child, she has moved more than 40 times in her life and loves "to travel, take pictures, and be in the sun." She quit her job as a video game designer to fulfill her love of travel, and when she was ready to settle in one place, she chose Asheville, in part because of the significant role that craftsmanship and artistry play in the area. She moved to Asheville just recently, driving from New York in a VW Gulf "with two cats, a puppy, and 30,000 bees" to a 100-year-old home in the countryside, the interior of which still shows its log cabin bones. Whitney installed her beehives—which are protected by an electric fence from the mama black bear and three cubs that often venture into the yard—and spent the first couple of months living in the house and completely renovating the kitchen.

As time allows, Whitney is hoping to return to her original purpose for learning to sew: creating a small wardrobe of versatile pieces for herself. Other creative pursuits include working on a graphic novel and continuing her ongoing home renovation. "I don't want any one of my interests to dominate my life," she explains. "That's what I find so frustrating with

social media. You have to look perfect, and you have to focus on one interest and make it your 'thing.' But what do we do when we can't be perfect? That's going to become a question for all of us in the social media age." ⌘

Whitney does all of her sewing on a vintage Singer sewing machine (above). Here, she models an unfinished version of the Fable Dress (right).

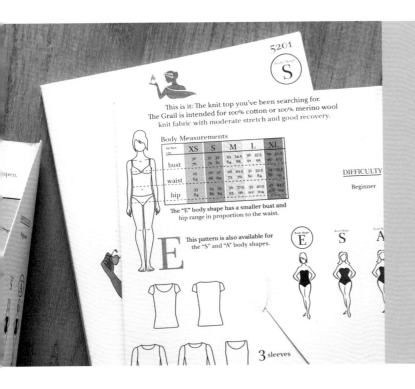

Vesta Patterns

Patternmaker: Whitney Hills

Website: vestapatterns.com

Products: The Grail (knit tee) and Fable Dress, each in three different body shapes

Maywood Totepack
by Ellie Lum of Klumhouse

At home around town, on campus, or rambling outdoors, the Maywood Totepack converts from tote to backpack seamlessly. Waxed canvas fabrics, leather straps and hardware, and an interior pocket that fits up to a 15" laptop make this totepack versatile, sturdy, and fun to sew. Learning how to work with leather and install rivets is not as difficult as it may seem and a great skill to add to your sewing repertoire - and, it gives your totepack a professional, finished look. All sewing can be accomplished on a home machine, and you won't believe how quickly it goes together!

Skill Level: Beginner-Advanced Beginner

Production Time: 4-6 hrs

MAYWOOD TOTE WAXED CANVAS MAKER KIT
Includes everything to make the Maywood Totepack, cut, prepped and ready to make! Fabric is cut to size and marked. Leather comes ready to add to your bag. Choose from eleven different colors of high quality waxed canvas, tan or black leather, and brass hardware. Order at www.klumhouse.com/maker-kits

MAYWOOD TOTE FINISHING KIT

You provide the fabric, we provide the rest! All the leather, zipper, and hardware a stitcher needs to make the Maywood Tote! All leather is cut to size, finished with elegant rounded ends, and pre-hole punched. Choose from tan leather or black leather. All hardware is brass. Order at www.klumhouse. com/maker-kits

SUPPLIES
Fabric:
* 1/2 yard fabric for pockets. Medium-heavyweight textile such as canvas, waxed canvas or denim.
* 1/2 yard fabric for liner. Medium-heavyweight textile such as canvas, waxed canvas or denim.
* 1/2 yard fabric for exterior and reinforcement fabric. Medium-heavyweight textile such as canvas, waxed canvas or denim.

Leather:
* 145" total length belting or tooling leather for straps. 6/7 oz or 7/8 oz leather strapped at 3/4" wide.

NOTIONS
Hardware:
* Double-cap rivets: 8-10 mm post length, 21 pcs (Note: These are quick-set rivets (also called Jiffy rivets or size 2204 rivets) that can be set with a hammer).
* O-Rings: , ¾" brass, 4 pcs
* Line 24 snap, 1 set
* 14" brass zipper

TOOLS
Sewing Tools:
Edge-stitch presser foot
Zipper foot
Denim needles
All-purpose thread
Scissors
Rotary cutter
Fabric marking tool
Quilting ruler
Straight pins
Craft Clips
Self-healing cutting mat

Leather and Hardware Tools:
Drive Punch or Rotary punch for rivets (3/32" or 2.5mm)
Drive Punch or Rotary punch for line 24 snap (5/32" or 4.0mm)
Hammer
Mallet
Anvil or hard smooth hammering surface
Cutting board
Line 24 snap hand setting tool

Optional- Industrial hand-press with corresponding dies for double cap rivets and line 24 snaps
Optional- 3/4" Round strap end punch

Need to source just the hardware or rivet setting tools? We got you covered! Handpicked high quality bag making tools and materials are available at www.klumhouse.com/supplies.

CUTTING AND MARKING
Pattern Measurements and Marking:
Exterior: 18 ½ " H x 17 ½ "W, cut 2
Lining: 18 ½ " H x 17 ½ "W, cut 2

Mark: Back of lining piece. Make a center mark on the right side of one 17 ½" long side (8 ¾" in from raw edge). Mark a 12" line across the 17 ½" long side at 2 ½" down from raw edge & centered. This will be your top of pocket placement mark.

On the bottom edge of the wrong side of both lining pieces, make marks 8" apart from center of fabric. These marks delineate the beginning and end of the Bag Turn-Out Gap.

Exterior Pocket: 17 ½ " H x 17 ½ "W, cut 1
Interior Pocket: 14 " H x 13 "W, cut 1

Reinforcement Fabric:
17 ½" x 2 ½", Cut 1
17 ½" x 5 ½", Cut 1

Leather Measurements, Marking, and Punching:

Leather Reinforcement Tabs: 2 5/8 " × ¾", cut 4
Mark & Punch: Holes, ½" in from each short edge, centered on ¾" width (2 holes in each tab).

O-ring Tabs: 2 5/8" × ¾", cut 4
Mark & Punch: Holes, ½" in from each short edge, centered on ¾" width (2 holes in each tab).

Leather Zipper Pull: 4 ½" × 3/4", cut 1
(For zipper slider with wide hole, otherwise cut 4 ½" × 1/4"). Holes 1 3/4" in from either side

Backpack Strap Band: 11" × ¾", cut 1
Mark & Punch: Holes 3/8" in & 2" in from either end and centered on the 3/4" width. 4 holes total.

Leather Washers for Line 24 snaps: Either 5/8" diameter round or square, cut 2.
Punch a hole 5/32" centered in each washer.

Backpack Strap Handle: 9" × 3/4" cut 1
Mark & Punch: ½" from either end, centered on 3/4" width.
Optional: To nicely finish the ends of your straps, cut each short end of leather with your choice of 3/4" leather strap end punch. We prefer using a round end punch.

Tote Straps: 35" × ¾", cut 1
Mark & Punch: Holes, ½" & 3" in from either end & centered on the ¾" width.

Bottom of Backpack Strap Reinforcement Tabs: 1 3/4" by 3/4", cut 2
Mark & Punch: Mark holes at 3/8" in from either end, centered on the 3/4" width.

Backpack Strap: 60" × 3/4", cut 1
Mark & Punch: Mark center of 60" length (30") on the backside of the leather. Then mark & punch 3 7/8" out from either side of the center (2 holes total).
Mark & Punch: Make marks 10 3/8" & 13" up from edges of backpack strap on the backside of the leather. Using the O-ring tab as a template, place it in between the 10 3/8" & 13" marks. Mark & punch.
Mark & Punch: Using the Bottom of Backpack Strap Reinforcement Tab as a template, place it flush with an end, then mark & punch. Repeat for other end (4 holes total).

REINFORCEMENT FABRIC

STEP 1: Center the right side of top reinforcement fabric over the wrong side of the exterior back fabric, aligning the top edge (17 ½" long side) of the top reinforcement fabric with the top edge (17 ½" long side) of the exterior fabric and pin.

STEP 2: Center the wrong side of bottom reinforcement fabric over the wrong side of the exterior back fabric, aligning the bottom edge of the bottom edge of the exterior fabric and pin.

STEP 3: Edgestitch all around all sides of both pieces of reinforcement fabric with a 1/8" seam allowance.

EXTERIOR POCKET

STEP 1: Make two Fold To lines across the top of the exterior pocket (the 17 ½'''' long side) towards the wrong side using a fabric marking chalk. One mark measures 1" down from the raw edge & the other measures 2 ½" down. Fold the fabric to meet the marks you created by finger pressing a ½" fold & then press a 1" fold to the wrong side, creating a 1" hem.
NOTE: Finger press waxed canvas. Do not iron waxed canvas. Wax melts!

STEP 2: Edgestitch the folded hem down.

STEP 3: Optional Snap Closure. See below to set the snap closure.

STEP 4: Center the right side of the exterior pocket over the right side of the exterior fabric, aligning the bottom of the pocket with the bottom of the exterior fabric and pin.

STEP 5: Stitch the sides and bottom of the exterior pocket onto the exterior fabric using an 1/8" seam allowance. TIP: Do this in one stitch, pivoting around the bottom corners.

NOTE: The top hem stitch might cause the pocket fabric to gather and be slightly smaller than the exterior piece. When stitching around the edges, measure your seam allowances against the fabric with the outermost edge.

STEP 6: Draw a line 3" up from the bottom edge of the pocket piece. Stitch along this line. (Note: This line will prevent items from slipping into the bottom portion of the pocket.)

OPTIONAL EXTERIOR POCKET SNAP
STEP 3:
Set the snap closure: On the right side of the top of the pocket, mark the center of the width (8 3/4" in from raw edge) and ½" down from top (centered on the hem). Punch a hole with a 5/32" drive punch or rotary punch through both pocket & exterior fabrics at the same time in the center where the marks intersect.

Set the snap.

Push the cap through the pocket from the exterior. Then on the other side of the fabric, push the cap through the leather washer, then attach the socket. Use a snap setter to join the two pieces, creating the male side of the snap.

On the exterior piece, slip the post through the leather washer and then through the fabric, again, using a snap setter, join the pieces together to create the female side of the snap.

TIP: For a full video tutorial on how to set a line 24 snap go to:
www.klumhouse.com/blog/set-snap

INTERIOR POCKET

STEP 1: Make two Fold To lines across the top of the interior pocket (the 13" long side) towards the wrong side using a fabric marking chalk. One mark measures 1" down from the raw edge and the other measures 1 ½" down. Fold the fabric to meet the marks you created by finger pressing a ½" fold, then press another ½" fold to the wrong side, creating a ½ " double-turn hem. (Note: Finger press waxed canvas. Do not iron waxed canvas. Wax melts!)

STEP 2: Edgestitch the folded hem down.

STEP 3: Make 1" Fold To marks on the three remaining sides of the interior pocket. Create a ½" fold towards the wrong side on the rest of the three sides. Align the top of the interior pocket with the top of pocket placement mark and pin the pocket right side up to the right side of the lining.

STEP 4: Edgestitch around both sides & the bottom of the interior pocket with a 1/8" seam allowance.

INSERTING THE ZIPPER

STEP 1: Mark the center of the zipper and the center of the front exterior piece on the top 17 ½" long side. Align the zipper center with the exterior front piece center mark, right sides together and pin or clip.

STEP 2: Working from the inside edges of the zipper tape, fold the beginning and end of the zipper tape at a right angle to meet the outside edges of the zipper tape. This will create nice finished ends of the zipper tape by tucking the ends within the bag.

TIP: Begin by creating a 1" long stitching line, at the beginning of the tape at a 1/8" seam allowance, back-stitch and then fold the zipper tape and stitch down. Or use Wash-Away-Wonder Tape to keep end of zipper tape folded while you stitch down. Do this at both ends.

STEP 3: Sew the zipper tape to the exterior piece using a 1/8" seam allowance. Remember to move the zipper head while stitching. When close to the zipper head, set the needle in the fabric halfway and completely lift the presser foot. This should leave enough clearance to pull the zipper head around the needle.

STEP 4: With back of the zipper face up, place the front lining piece (the one without

73

the interior pocket), right side down. Stitch down from one end of the fabric to the other end of the fabric, using a 1/4" seam allowance. (Note: The zipper should be sandwiched in between the exterior & liner fabrics.)

TIP: Remember to move the zipper pull while stitching.

STEP 5: In preparation for sewing the other side of the zipper, flip the exterior and liner fabric to the other side to reveal the zipper. Align the sides of the exterior back fabric with the sides of the front fabric, right sides together and clip or pin fabric to zipper.
REPEAT STEPS 1-4 TO STITCH OTHER SIDE OF ZIPPER.

INSTALLING THE BACKPACK STRAPS
Installing the Backpack Strap Band
Step 1: Make a center mark on the back of the bag at the top. Then draw a 11" long line 1" down from the top edge of the fabric (where the fabric connects to the zipper). Make small perpendicular marks on each end of the 11" line. This will be the placement mark for the top of the Backpack Strap Band.

Use the holes in the Backpack Strap Band as a template to make the rivet placement marks. Using a chalk pencil, and the holes in the leather as a template, mark through the leather to create rivet placement marks.

Remove the Backpack Strap Band and use a leather punch or drive punch (3/16") to create holes through both layers of fabric (the exterior and the reinforcement fabric) at the rivet placement marks.

Take two sets of rivets (post & cap). Insert the posts into the Backpack Strap Reinforcement Tab holes from the right side of the leather. Next, insert the posts into the bag from the backside of the fabric. Then place the Backpack Strap Band right side up through these rivets and put the caps on the posts, sandwiching the Backpack Strap Leather and fabric in between the rivet heads.

Set the rivets (see Special Techniques).

Installing the Backpack Strap Handle
Step 2: Take four sets of rivets (post & cap). Insert the posts into the leather Backpack Handle from the right side. Next insert the post into the holes near the center of the strap (7 3/4" out from either side of the center) from the right side. Put the rivet caps on the posts, sandwiching the Backpack Strap leather and Backpack Handle leather in between the rivet heads.

Set the rivets.

Note: The Backpack Strap Handle will not lay flush with the Backpack Strap, allowing for ease when the strap is curved.

Threading the Backpack Strap Through the Band
Step 3: Thread each end of the Backpack Strap through each side of the Backpack Strap Band from the top down. The Backpack Strap should easily slide through the slots on either end of the Backpack Strap Band. Pull each end of the Backpack Strap until the O-ring placement holes are below the Backpack Strap Band.

INSTALLING THE BACKPACK STRAPS
Attach O-rings to Backpack Strap
Step 4: Take two sets of rivets (post & cap). Insert the posts into the Backpack Strap O-ring placement holes from the back side of the leather. Next, working with one rivet at a time, insert the post into the O-ring leather tab from the back side. Then connect a cap to the post. Thread an O-ring through the leather tab before placing the other hole onto a post and secure it with a cap. Set the rivets.

REPEAT FOR OTHER SIDE

Installing the bottom ends of the Backpack Strap
Step 5: Working on the back exterior fabric only, and starting on the left side, measure 4" up from bottom seam and 1 ½" in from side seam and make a mark. Measure 5" up from the bottom seam and 2" in from the side seam and make another mark. These will be your rivet placement marks to attach the bottom of the backpack straps.

REPEAT FOR BOTTOM RIGHT SIDE OF BACK EXTERIOR.

Note: Do not set the leather into the lining fabric. Work only with the exterior fabric.

STEP 6: Cut the rivet placement marks out of the fabric using a drive punch and cutting board.

REPEAT FOR RIGHT SIDE.

STEP 7: Take four sets of rivets (post & cap). Insert the posts into the Bottom of Backpack Strap Reinforcement Tab holes from the right side of the leather. Next insert the posts into the bag from the back side of the exterior fabric. Then place the Backpack Strap leather right side up through these rivets from the exterior of the tote. Put the rivet caps on the posts, sandwiching the Backpack Strap leather and fabric in between the rivet heads. Set the rivets.

SEWING THE BAG TOGETHER
STEP 1: Open the zipper ¾ of the way. Bring lining pieces right sides together and align sides and bottoms. Make sure that the Bag Turn-Out Gap marks at the bottom of the lining are visible. A gap in stitching that is 8" long should be left on the bottom edge of the lining in order to turn the bag right side out.

STEP 2: Nest the seam allowances on the top seams of the bag and clip in place (the seam that attaches the exterior and lining together). Pin around the entire outer edge of the bag except for the opening in the bottom of the lining piece where the bag will be turned right side out. Using a fabric marking tool and a quilting ruler, draw 2 ½" x 2 ½" squares on all four corners of the bag, forming boxes in each corner. Two sides of each box are the raw edges of the fabric. These boxes will be cut out later to form boxed corners.

Start sewing at one gap marking and end at the other gap marking, using a 1/2" seam allowance. While sewing, backstitch over every box line in all corners. This will keep the side seam from unraveling when you cut out the squares.

BOXING THE CORNERS
STEP 1: Cut out the 2 ½" x 2 ½" boxes at all 4 corners on the chalk cut lines.

STEP 2: Grab the inside corners of one box and pull them both out simultaneously, creating a boxed corner. Nest the seam allowances. To avoid bulk, nest the side seam and bottom seam into each other by pressing one of the seams towards one side and the opposite seam to the opposite side. Pin or clip. Stitch together using a 1/2" seam allowance. Repeat this step for the remaining 3 corners.

NOTE: Don't be afraid to boss the fabric into position to get it to fold at the corner points and create a straight edge across the seam. Otherwise, the fabric wants to curve, and not lay straight.

SEWING THE BAG TURN-OUT GAP
STEP 1: Turn the bag right side out through the gap in the lining. Turn the seam allowance in the gap in towards the wrong side of lining and pin. Edgestitch the gap in the lining shut using a 1/8" seam allowance. Extend the stitch slightly beyond the opening in the beginning and end.

TIP: Consider switching to thread that matches your lining.

STEP 2: Stuff the lining into the exterior bag.

NOTE: Make sure to pull up the top corners of the bag near the ends of the zipper, ensuring that the top seam rests at the very top of the bag.

INSTALLING THE TOTE STRAP
STEP 1: Make a center mark on the front of the bag at the top. Mark 3 ½" out from either side of the center mark. Then mark 3/4" out from both 3 ½" marks. Use the O-ring

leather tab as a template to make rivet placement marks on the fabric. Place a 2 ½" x 3/4" O-ring leather tab in between the chalk marks on the fabric and ½" down from the top of the fabric. Using a chalk pencil and the holes in the leather as a template, mark through the leather to create rivet placement marks on the fabric. Punch holes in the fabric at rivet placement marks.

STEP 2: Take two sets of rivets (post & cap). Insert the posts into the Tote Strap Reinforcement Tab holes from the right side of the leather, then through the lining and the exterior fabric from the inside of the bag. Next, working with one rivet at a time, insert the post into the O-ring leather tab from the back side. Then connect a cap to the post. Thread an O-ring through the leather tab before placing the other hole onto a post and secure it with a cap. Set the rivets.

Note: If done correctly, the O-ring should be threaded through the O-ring Leather Tab on the exterior of the bag and a leather reinforcement tab should be on the interior of the bag.

REPEAT FOR OTHER SIDE

STEP 3: Attach the Tote Strap. Take one rivet set and insert the post into one of the holes at the end of the tote strap from the right side. Thread the tote strap through an O-ring. Then insert the post into the other hole at the end of the tote strap. Set the rivet.

REPEAT FOR OTHER SIDE

INSTALLING THE ZIPPER PULL
Thread the leather pull through the zipper slider. Align the two punched holes on the leather pull, wrong sides together. Insert a post into the zipper holes from the right side and connect a cap. Set the rivet.

SPECIAL TECHNIQUES

Cut the rivet placement marks. Use a rotary leather punch to cut rivet holes. Alternatively, use a drive punch on top of a cutting board with a mallet to create holes at the rivet placement marks.

TIP: For a full video tutorial on how to set a rivet go to: www.klumhouse.com/blog/set-rivet

Set the rivets. Place them directly on an anvil or other hard hammering surface, and use a hammer to secure the rivets together. (Note: A industrial snap press fitted with the correct dies can also be used to set the double-cap rivets.)

ADVENTURE TIME!

A PDF version of this pattern, with in-process and how-to photos, at www.byhandserial.com/maywood-instructions (enter code "MaywoodTotepack")

In the Kitchen: Spring Clouds

Some call them Pavlovas while others call them baked meringues. Whatever you call them, these lemony, fruity, light and crispy confections will be a delight for your spring entertaining. Topped with fresh fruit and tiny edible blossoms, they are like puffy spring clouds for your table.

Note: Any mildly flavored edible flower blossom will work as the finishing touch for this recipe. Just be sure that the flowers are free from pesticides. Some of the loveliest are violas, as pictured. You can also use (among others): apple blossoms, borage, cornflower, dianthus, nasturtium, and rose. Always be sure that whatever blossoms you are using are safely edible before using in any recipe. Local farmers' markets can be a great resource for finding edible blooms.

INGREDIENTS
Meringues:
3 large egg whites
1 teaspoon vanilla extract
¼ teaspoon cream of tartar
Dash of salt
2/3 cup sugar

Topping:
Lemon curd (commercially prepared or homemade)
Mascarpone cheese
Raspberries or other fruit
Edible flower blossoms

DIRECTIONS:

Preheat oven to 250°.

Separate the whites from the yolks of three large eggs. Be careful not to get any yolks in with the whites. The yolks can be set aside and used later for a chocolate mousse or other custard treat. Let the whites sit at room temperature for 20-30 minutes.

In a large mixing bowl, combine egg whites, vanilla, cream of tartar, and salt. Mix on medium speed until frothy. Increase speed to high, and add sugar one tablespoon at a time, beating thoroughly to incorporate between each spoonful. Continue beating until stiff, glossy peaks form, at least 5 minutes. *Hint: Stiff peaks (see photo) mean that when you pull the beater out and turn it upright, the peak doesn't fold back on itself. Don't over-beat, though. Once you get to stiff peaks, stop.

You can pipe the meringues out onto a parchment paper-lined baking sheet using a piping set or bag with the corner cut off, or you can scoop them out using two spoons, which gives a more rustic look (as pictured). Create meringue circles about 2-½ inches across with a flat-ish or slightly concave top. That is where you will put the toppings, so the top does not have to look perfect. The meringues will not spread as they cook, so feel free to put them as close as you want—without touching—on the tray.

Bake at 250° for 45 minutes, then turn off the oven and let the meringues rest there several hours or overnight. The longer they stay in the oven, the lighter and crispier they will be. Meringues can be made ahead and kept, covered, at room temperature for up to several days before assembling the clouds.

Topping: In a medium bowl, mix ½ cup lemon curd with ½ cup mascarpone cheese until smooth and well blended. Spread 1 tablespoon of the lemon-cheese mixture on each meringue. Top with berries and a single flower blossom. Serve immediately.

Yield: about 16 meringues

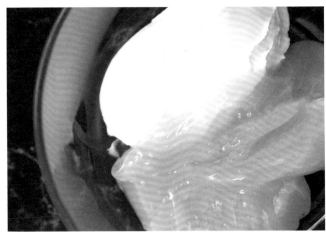

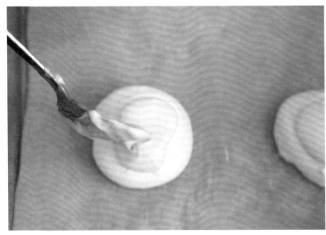

Surface Design: Cloth Fiber Workshop

Cloth Fiber Workshop founder Barbara Zaretsky emphasizes that the Workshop's classes "build community and make sure that people are still being creative with textiles, by learning and using old techniques in a new way." A wide variety of classes are taught by guest instructors throughout the year, with a focus on plant dyes and surface design. Indigo, shibori, and embroidery are also featured in upcoming classes.

Barbara also creates under her own label, BZ Design, which focuses on textile arts using natural dyes and sustainable fabrics such as hemp, silk, and linen. Barbara has been fascinated by fabrics since she was a child, which led to the study of textile arts, weaving and surface design in school and a career in graphic design before quitting her "day job" a decade ago to pursue her artistic career full-time. Barbara developed her focus on "classical" dyes and processes because "I'm concerned about how the process affects the planet, my health, and my customers' health."

Barbara uses traditional methods of block printing to achieve a modern aesthetic. "When I took a natural dyeing class, I was able to achieve the color palette I was looking for." She loves the randomness that results from using natural materials, and the minimalist effect she can achieve by concentrating on the dyeing process and the colors that natural dyes create. "It creates an interest that's new every time," she explains. Some of her textile arts become shawls, scarves, and occasionally clothing, while others are sewn into home decor—wall textiles, pillows, and table runners. BZ Design textiles are sold at the Cloth Fiber Workshop studio, and online, as well as at several regional shows each year. ⌘

Cloth Fiber Workshop and BZ Design

Websites: clothfiberworkshop.com and bzdesign.biz

Address: 191 Lyman St., Studio 104, Asheville, N.C.

Phone: 828.505.2958

Workshops: Working with shibori, indigo, embroidery, natural plant dyes, screen printing, and surface design

BZ Design Products: Pillows, wall textiles, table runners, scarves, and shawls

The Mabry Mill is one of the most photographed sites on the Blue Ridge Parkway.

Where to Learn: Penland School of Crafts

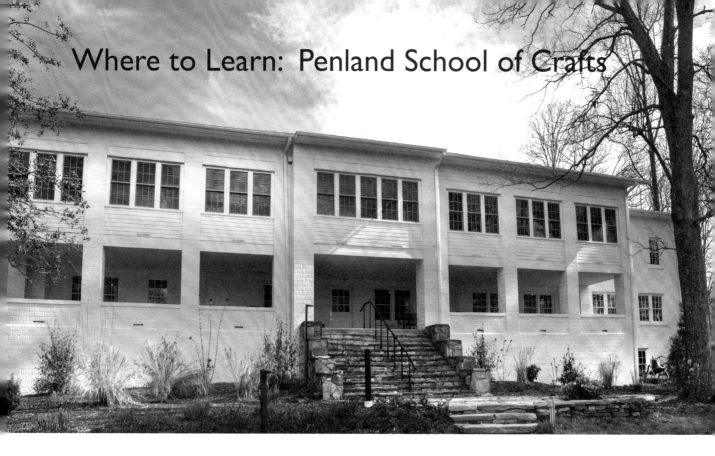

Most of us squeeze chances to create into small spaces of our busy days. We knit a few rows while watching a child's sporting event. We manage one or two steps of a sewing project each morning before the household wakes up. We embroider a small section during a lunch break, or on the train, or late at night before falling asleep. All the while, we dream of a place where we could totally immerse ourselves in making, without outside distractions or obligations—time to talk with other makers, learn new techniques, and enjoy the slow, steady pace of creating by hand.

Penland School of Crafts fulfills all of these dreams. Located on 400 isolated acres on the top of a mountain in western North Carolina, it offers the opportunity to learn in one-week or eight-week sessions during the fall and spring or two-week sessions during the summer from some of the best artists and instructors in the country. "Penland serves people whose lives are focused on making things and those who engage with craft as an enhancement to their lives. Everybody learns from each other. The only prerequisite for participation is a passion for making," summarizes the School's brochure. Each session consists of demonstrations, lectures, individual studio work, discussions and critiques, and field trips. Classes are held in the morning and the afternoon, but the studios are open all the time, and students can work whenever they like. Although they vary from session to session, classes are typically offered in clay, glass, iron, metals, photo, wood, printmaking, letterpress, textiles, painting, books, and "specials," many of which involve mixed media work. Most workshops are listed as "all levels," and welcome dedicated students from beginning to advanced.

Students live, work, and eat on campus, which offers the opportunity to create a unique learning community without outside distractions. The Penland handbook notes that "total-immersion

85

workshops are a uniquely effective educational method … that supports craft traditions while reshaping craft in the context of the contemporary world." All of the classes are taught by studio artists or college faculty who teach at Penland for a limited period of time as guest instructors. This allows the school to continuously offer classes with new content or areas of focus. Communications & Marketing Manager Robin Dreyer tells me that the students are pretty consistently one-third under the age of 30, with another third over the age of 60. Women typically outnumber men two to one, regardless of the age category. Penland works hard to make classes accessible to anyone who is interested in learning there, and a wide variety of partial, full, and work study scholarships are available. It also offers short-term residency programs of one to six weeks in the "quiet season" of January and February, which provide a small number of artists with an opportunity to "work independently in an inspiring and collegial setting."

The School first opened in 1929 as a weaving school for local women, founded by Lucy Morgan. The original building still stands, but most of the studio buildings have been recently constructed or renovated. As a result, each of the major media areas have beautifully constructed dedicated areas, with high ceilings and lots of natural light. The textiles studio houses a fleet of floor looms, and accommodates an almost endless variety of classes. It has a large dye kitchen, long tables for sewing and pattern construction, and other spaces that can be used for leather work, quilting, knitting, felting, or shibori, to name just a

LITHO INKS

few. Our tour fell in the middle of an eight-week shoemaking class, and we wandered through the work tables filled with shoes in all stages of construction, marveling at the variety of styles and designs that the students were experimenting with.

The quiet, bucolic setting, the state-of-the-art studios and tools, and the lack of interruptions from the outside world all create an environment where anyone who loves making has the opportunity to delve deeper into an area—whether well-known or unexplored—and fully enjoy not only what is produced, but the process itself. At the end of our tour, we watched the students who were just finishing their one-week session participate in a show-and-tell, sharing their triumphs and challenges, showing their completed artwork and chatting about the work and the learning that went into its creation. The big studio buzzed with excitement and laughter, and it was powerful to watch artists of all ages, abilities, and backgrounds find common ground and meaning in work they had created with their own hands. In a busy, distractible modern age, Penland provides an opportunity to makers that is truly unique and meaningful. ⌘

Penland School of Crafts

Website: penland.org

Address: 67 Doras Trail, Penland, N.C.

Phone: 828.765.2359

Classes: Eight-week fall and spring programs, one-week intensives, and two-week summer sessions

By Hand Author and Photographer

Andrea Hungerford loves knitting for both the solitude it provides and the community it builds. Most all of her remaining time is spent with her three teenage daughters, who have taught her to navigate and even occasionally embrace the crazy chaos of everyday life. Her summertime home away from home is the San Juan Islands, and her favorite place to scuba dive is Turks & Caicos, where she once swam with a whale shark. She hates to cook but loves to bake, and learns to navigate any new city she visits by locating the best bakery in town and going from there. She has cultivated a large and unwieldy garden at her home in the countryside, and loves to pick lilacs and peonies in the spring, sweet cherry tomatoes in the summer, and pink, red, and orange dahlias in the fall. She cares passionately about the environment and believes that there is no greater cause than protecting the natural world for future generations.

Karen DeWitz couldn't knit to save her life, but she's enchanted by the art of it all and loves having the chance to see so many gorgeous creations crafted by makers around the country. Not to be completely left out of the making party, Karen dabbles in other creative pursuits—most obviously, photography, but also jewelry-making and the occasional drawing or written story. She loves the photographic challenge of capturing the feel of a soft alpaca yarn or the grain of rich leather using just light and focus. Traveling to amazing new places with Andrea to create images for By Hand Serial is a professional dream, and not just because Karen's profound love of coffee pairs so well with Andrea's obsession with bakeries. Karen lives in the woods just outside of Oregon City with her husband, teenage son (whose older brother is away at college), and a rambunctious fluffy dog.

Up Next . . .

Upcoming issues of **By Hand** will feature different makers' communities around the United States, and the world. If you have suggestions for an artist or maker, a knitting store or small business, or anything unique, we'd love to hear from you! Do you know of a makers' community that you think we should profile? If so, let us know! Email us at: info@byhandserial.com.

You can also find us on:
Ravelry at www.ravelry.com/groups/by-hand-serial
Facebook at www.facebook.com/byhandserial
Instagram at www.instagram.com/byhandserial

Below: Wildflowers blooming on the rolling hills of Virginia.
Back Cover: Grafitti art along the railroad tracks in Asheville's River Arts District.